Writing for College

Gary Boyer
Keuka College

Illustrated by
John Locke

WRITING FOR COLLEGE.
Copyright @ 2013 by Gary Boyer.
ISBN 978-1-304-10005-4.

For Kathy and Emma

ntroduction

Like students everywhere, many Keuka College students struggle with writing. In our Accelerated Studies for Adults Program, this struggle is aggravated by the same forces that challenge all working adults in school—especially in accelerated programs: many of them have been out of college for 10, 15, 20 or more years; their college writing skills are at best rusty; they have become oriented to writing for work, a very different skill set and one not all that conducive to success in college. And in an accelerated program, nearly all assessment of student learning is done through writing and oral presentation—the pressure is on, and there's no time to ease into it.

In July of 2010, I was fortunate enough to be asked to fill the new position of ASAP Academic Skills Counselor, with the mandate to address these challenges and to provide writing assistance to some 900 students in 7 degree programs (undergraduate Social Work, Nursing, Criminal Justice, and Management; and graduate Nursing, Management, and Criminal Justice).

One of the first steps I took in that role was to initiate a weekly writing tip that is sent via email blast to all ASAP students, faculty, and staff every Monday morning. The series, titled *Wordworks,* has a threefold mission: 1. to provide real advice that can improve student writing immediately, 2. to proactively reach out to students, rather than simply waiting for them to call, and 3. to publicize the fact that we have a Writing Support Center.

Wordworks has, I am happy to report, been well received. Several readers have asked whether the series could be published in book form. So here it is.

I have arranged the weekly tips in the order in which they appeared. There's no real reason to read them in order, though, just as there's no real reason to read all of them. I have provided a Subject Index at the back of the book to assist readers interested in finding something specific.

Last, but very far from least, how glad and grateful I am that my friend and colleague, John Locke, offered to art direct this project, and even gladder that he suggested including some of his wonderful cartoons! I know you will enjoy at least that much of this book. Thank you, John.

ndex of Topics

What A Difference A Title Makes

We have all been around the block enough times to know how important it is to make a good first impression. And, because it's the first thing your reader encounters in your paper, making a good first impression is the job of your **Title**. So it's worth a bit of effort to make it a good one.

- The title should be the very last thing you write. That's because a good title encapsulates or comments on what's in the paper
- You can certainly use a title like "Economics Research Paper #2," but that doesn't really get your reader very interested in reading on. Try to make your title a little more fun. Good ways to do this are:
  - Use a popular cliché or well known song lyric—a paper on the growth of Community College enrollments, for example, might be titled "Stairway to Heaven" or, perhaps, "Running With the Pack."
  - Read through the paper itself. I guarantee you will find a phrase that will make a good title.
  - Simply state the topic: "Community College Enrollment Growth."
  - In all of these options you might wish to follow the "catchy" title with a colon and a more explanatory phrase, thus:

"Stairway to Heaven: Growing Numbers of Adults Pursue Associates Degrees to Enhance Job Prospects."

Of course, you may find a way to come up with a good title that works better for you than these suggestions. The main thing is to TITLE EVERYTHING! And make that first impression as good as you can.

#2: Build In Some Do-Nothing Time

In an accelerated program like ASAP, it can seem as if time is the commodity always in shortest supply. And yet time away from your course paper can be the difference between good and excellent.

When you work on a paper, especially a research paper, you really must immerse yourself in it. You work on it every spare minute; you wake up at three in the morning thinking about it. That kind of immersion, while necessary, does have the side effect of making it impossible for you to read your work objectively. You know what it's supposed to say; you understand the relationships of the parts and pieces intimately; you think it's pretty much perfect.

That's when you need to save your document and do something else—or do nothing—for as long a time as you can afford.

And, guaranteed, when you return to your work after a couple of days, a day, even a few hours, you will see things that need to be improved, omitted, rewritten—and you will have a much better product to turn in.

That won't happen, however, unless you plan on it and build it in to your schedule from the beginning.

Hooked on Phonics

#3: The Passive Voice

When we read, we can most easily grasp the meaning when the writer has expressed things actively. That means that sentences in which the subject (some person or thing) *does* something are much clearer, easier to follow, and more interesting to read than any other arrangement.

In another kind of sentence, the subject does not act, but is the recipient of an action. Those are the sentences we refer to as being written in "The Passive Voice." There are times, to be sure, when you'll express yourself in the passive voice, but better not too often, and *never* without making a conscious decision to do so.

Let's be clear: the passive voice is not *wrong*, but it is usually boring and can often leave the reader wondering, as in a pulp mystery, *Whodunnit?*

Here's what we're talking about. These sentences are in the passive voice:
1. **Quantities of toxic chemicals were lost.**
2. **The concerto was performed to perfection.**
3. **The membrane was shown to be permeable under certain conditions.**

In sentence #1 there would seem to be serious culpability at issue: somebody lost those chemicals, but the sentence does not tell us who. Sentence #2 fails to give credit to whomever gave the audience real pleasure. Sentence #3, on the other hand, probably should be written in the passive voice as it shouldn't matter who observed this or conducted the experiment; the results should be the same regardless.

So, when your sentences are written in the passive voice (like this one), you ought to be able to explain why.

Those Pesky Commas: No Splices, Please!

This week's tip is in response to a student (you know who you are!) who wrote, "I could use some help with a refresher course in how and when to use commas."

Of all punctuation marks, commas seem to cause the most confusion. Either they, sneakily, find their, seemingly useful, way into every nook, corner, and cranny of your writing or they don't show up at all even when they could be of real assistance in making sense of things.

Consider using commas to join together two complete thoughts while avoiding the dreaded "comma splice."

So . . .

You might wish to emphasize the relationship between two thoughts:

Everybody arrived before 6:00. Class started on time.

One way to do it would be to use a comma and a conjunction (and, but, yet, or, nor), thus:

Everybody arrived before 6:00, and class started on time.

You could also decide not to use the conjunction, but in that case you can't use the comma either; you must use a semicolon.

Everybody arrived before 6:00; class started on time.

A third option might be to emphasize the cause and effect relationship by using "therefore."

Everybody arrived before 6:00; therefore class started on time.
(Notice that "therefore" is not a conjunction; so you still need the semicolon. The same goes for words like "however," "nevertheless," and "in any case".)

In weeks to come, we'll have lots more on commas; so stay tuned. In the meantime, check out Lewis Thomas' wonderful essay "Notes On Punctuation." You can find it online.

Ego Confusion

All through the day, I me mine
I me mine, I me mine
All through the night, I me mine
I me mine, I me mine.
—George Harrison

Thanks to Dr. Janet Mance, Program Administrator, Nursing, for suggesting that we ought to do a Writing Tip on the "I – Me" problem.

We choose the word we use to refer to ourselves, "I" or "me", depending on its role in the sentence. If I refer to myself as the subject (or "doer" of the action) I choose "I"; whereas, if I am the recipient of the action, I choose "me".

I studied for two hours.

My professor chose me to lead the discussion.

So far, so good. Things begin to go wrong when I team up with somebody else.

Me and Bill studied for two hours.

My professor chose Janet and I to lead the discussion.

Both of these are wrong. But somehow "Janet and me" doesn't sound as formal. Bottom line: you would <u>never</u> say, "My professor chose I to lead the discussion." Just as you would never say, "Me studied for two hours."

Hint: Read the sentence without the "and partner" part and you can't go wrong.

Also, resist the temptation to sound more sophisticated by using "myself" when you really mean "me".

"I spent the afternoon talking to myself," is fine.

"As for myself, I just don't get it." is not fine.
Make it "As for me . . . "

What's It All About?

It would be impossible to overstate the importance of making a good beginning to a piece of writing. A crucial part of that good beginning—in all writing, but especially in academic writing—is the Thesis Statement.

When we read, we expect that the writer will let us know very early on what the subject is and what we are in for. Certainly, the title begins to do that job, by getting us to start reading in the first place. But it is the Introduction and particularly the Thesis Statement that give us the wherewithal to make sense of what follows.

At its most essential, a Thesis Statement has three functional parts: it announces the subject; it advises of the writer's attitude or intention; and it lays out the writer's method.

For example:

Taking courses online is an attractive option because you can work when you want to, work from home, and get the undivided attention of the instructor.

If you read this statement, you would know pretty much what will follow. Wouldn't you?

Or in this one:

Absolute loyalty, unconditional love, and just the right amount of chaos: that's what you get from having a dog in your family.

The writer has promised to expand on three general areas relating to the benefits of dog ownership. And, having been prepared, you will be all the more delighted to see just how he or she pays off the promise.

(You will by now have noticed that another way of describing the Thesis Statement might be that it is kind of a one-sentence version of the whole essay.)

Months after the death of his camel,
Ahmed was still in de Nile.

Words to Watch For, Part I

Certain words just seem to cause problems for us. So it's probably a good idea to have those in mind when we are revising and editing what we have written. Below you'll find a few that are particularly problematic.

As you read through the draft of your essay, keep your eyes peeled in case you have erroneously written:

Everyday for every day

"Everyday" means "ordinary", as in, "This is my *everyday* Bills cap; I wear my new Bills cap only on game days." But, more and more, I'm seeing folks write "everyday" when they really mean "today, tomorrow, the day after, etc." or "every day".

Imply for infer

The writer or speaker *implies*; the reader or listener *infers*. It's that simple.

Lead for led

This one has begun to crop up in recent years, for some reason. "Led" is the past tense of "lead" (rhymes with "bleed"). "Lead" (rhymes with "bed") is the heavy metal that Superman uses to protect himself from Kryptonite.

Loosing for **losing**

I suspect that this is probably just a spelling problem that spell check won't catch. (Lots of those, aren't there?) Something in us wants to type "oo" for that long "o" sound.

Then for **than**

Here's another one that's way more frequent then (oops!) it ought to be. I imagine it's because, in conversation at least, we pronounce them both the same. (Note: I spotted this error in a *New York Times* online story. By the next morning they had, of course, fixed it. It can happen to anybody.)

Could of for **could have**

English teachers everywhere have been tearing out their hair over this one for decades, at least. But it's still alive and well. Again, I'm sure the error comes from the way we speak in conversation: "could've" sounds much more like "could of" than it does like "could have".

#8: Writing for Your Reader

The most obvious things, the things we most take for granted, are sometimes the most important. We overlook their fundamental importance because they are just that: fundamental. This week, we'll consider one of those: the most important person in your writer's world . . . your reader.

When it's midnight and you're straining your intellectual muscles to the limit to finish that research paper, it can be easy to forget the most obvious fact about writing. Except for diaries and journals, you don't write for yourself; you write for someone else to read. Keeping that fact in mind, though, will profoundly affect how well you succeed.

So . . .

1. Make It Clear Where You're Going

When you write, you see all aspects of your work in your mind's eye. Having planned, researched, and thought, you understand entirely how all the ideas, bits of evidence, major and minor points, examples, and citations fit together. Your reader, on the other hand, has an entirely different point of view. He or she encounters your writing from the beginning and moves word by word to the conclusion. That simple fact emphasizes how important it is to start by letting your reader know your subject, its context, your attitude, and—in general—the method you will use.

(A hint here: for whatever reason, we all like to make our last sentences real zingers, to slam home our point. Because of that, you will find that, more often than not, your paper will be improved greatly if you make that last sentence your first sentence. Try it, it really works.)

2. Assume That Your Reader Knows Next To Nothing About Your Topic

Even if you think of your instructor as your reader (She surely knows more about this than I do!), it's still better to over-explain than to under-explain. Your writing will be clearer; it will be much more likely that your reader gets your point, less likely that your writing will be vague or easily misconstrued.

Some specifics:

- Always spell out acronyms the first time you use them in an essay.
- As much as possible, avoid professional jargon. It's probably impossible to avoid it altogether, but it will be worth the effort.
- Except for the most general knowledge, don't assume that your reader will understand historical or cultural references. (Everybody knows Frank Sinatra, Bob Dylan, and The Beatles; not everybody knows Dropkick Murphys, Tony Joe White, Lil Wayne, or The White Stripes).

3. Give a Thought to Presentation

A piece of writing makes an impression before you even begin to read it.

So make yours look clean and inviting. Use white space, numbers, bullet lists. Think about subheads for the sections of your paper. (This is one of the advantages of APA, by the way; it pretty well forces you to format things.

#9: Are We In Agreement . . . ?

The grammar we all learned in elementary school—at least as I remember it—came through as a lot of rules for rules' sake. Somebody (the Grand Emperor of English Class?) promulgated them for reasons unknown to us—following them was just one of those things you had to do as a kid.

Looking at grammar functionally, as a tool, we can see that what it really does is to help us satisfy our reader's expectation of consistency. If we start out writing, as here, speaking as "we", our reader has a right to expect that we won't suddenly shift to "I" or "you".

It can get sticky, though, especially when we get into the area of **Agreement** (i.e., consistency) in **Number**. The basics here are nearly self-evident. In "Subject-Verb Agreement," consistency demands that a singular subject gets a singular verb; plural subjects get plural verbs.

"ASAP **classes are held** one night a week at locations throughout Central and Western New York. Each weekly **meeting lasts** four hours."

. . . even when there are lots of words in the way!

"The real **pleasure** of college study—dealing with ideas, making friends, challenging beliefs—**sticks** with us long after we graduate."

The fun begins when we get into "**Pronoun-Antecedent Agreement**". In this sentence:

"Many employees have seen their **roles** evolve into something different than **they** were less than a year ago."

"They" is the pronoun the writer used to avoid repeating the word "roles" (its antecedent).

Then gender gets into the act. Many of us are tempted to handle things this way:

"Each **student** needs to develop **their** own topic proposal."

But "their" is clearly plural while "student" is singular. The problem is, of course, that students can be male or female, and here we don't know which.

When some of us were young, the Grand Emperor suggested that we simply use "his" rather than "their" in a case like this. The entirely preposterous rationale was that the male pronoun stands for all people. Please.

So, how about:

"Each **student** needs to develop **his or her** own topic proposal."

That works, even if it's a little wordy. Or we could make the whole thing plural:

"Students need to develop **their** own topic proposal**s**."

That also works. (Note that "proposal" has to become plural, too, since the students are presumably not all working on the same proposal.)

Or, avoid the whole problem:

"Topic proposal development is each student's individual responsibility."

That just might be the best choice.

What's The Idea?

Have you ever found yourself sitting in front of your computer having the general idea of what you want to write, but not quite knowing where to start?   Here are two techniques that work for people to get them started. Give them a try; see if one works for you.

What they have in common is that they tend to help us learn from ourselves, in a sense. That is, they provide ways to discover what we didn't think we knew.

Freewriting

A clock is the most important tool in freewriting. The alarm clock on your cellphone is ideal.

The process is simple: set your alarm for five, ten, or fifteen minutes (no more). Then begin to write whatever comes into your head. Don't stop; don't read what you have written; just keep writing. If you can't think of anything to write, write, "I can't think of anything to write." It need not make sense; no capital letters or punctuation required. Don't worry about making sentences. Write on your computer or write with a pen or pencil—whatever suits you.

When the alarm goes off, stop. Read. I'll be surprised if there's not something there you really like.

Listmaking

I think of listmaking as personal brainstorming. You know the rules in a brainstorming session: there are no bad ideas; there is no editing; everything gets recorded.

Begin your list with a word that has something to do with your topic. Below it write a second word, a third below the second, and so on. Soon you will have a column of words. Keep going until you feel like you have enough, until you start to see patterns and to get ideas. That could be ten or twenty words; it could be several pages. You will find yourself combining words into phrases that you like, and those combinations will suggest others to you in turn.

Note: some folks have suggested that this works best with pen and paper. They even suggest turning lined paper on its side and writing words and phrases at random all over the page, across the lines.

One more thing: If you decide to try one of these techniques, make sure you save the document until you're all finished with your paper. You never know when something you freewrote or listed will be just the thing on page 7.

#11:

Reading about Writing

Probably the best answer to the question, "What can I do to improve my writing?" is, "Read." Reading (pretty much anything: *The Auburn Citizen*, Dave Barry's humor, e.e.cummings' poetry, Harry Potter) builds a sense of how sentences work and of how our language sounds.

But this week I want to mention three books that can go far beyond that kind of help. These books are about writing, especially writing better.

1. *Writing for Results in Business, Government, The Sciences, and The Professions*, by David Ewing

This book was written long before the internet came into being, so its examples of correspondence (letters and memos) are a little out of date for most of us. That's really a small quibble, though. I know of no other book that approaches writing so pragmatically and offers advice that works so well.

A professor at Harvard Business School, Ewing cares only about what works. He tells the reader what that is and explains why it is so. He has no patience for rambling, useless words, or soft-pedaling— because they don't get the job done.

2. *Eats, Shoots, and Leaves*, by Lynne Truss

A bestseller about commas and apostrophes? Who'd a thunk it? But in 2004, this book was a phenomenon. Very funny, very sharp, and without mercy for the violators of basic punctuation and grammar, Ms. Truss is the fussiest, friendliest, and funniest English teacher imaginable.

And while you're laughing, you're also thinking hard about the real power those little curlicues of type can wield if used well and the real potential for disaster if not.

3. *The Elements of Style*, by William Strunk Jr. and E. B. White

A mere 105 pages long, including the very useful Index, "Strunk and White", as it's usually called, is THE single most important book on the fundamentals of writing well.

The book was born at Cornell University in the very early years of the Twentieth Century, when an English professor there, William Strunk, wrote down his lectures and had them printed up in what he (and everyone else at Cornell) called "the little book". E.B. White, who achieved fame as a writer for *The New Yorker* magazine and as the author of *Charlotte's Web*--and who had actually sat in Professor Strunk's English class in 1919--edited the book for the publisher Macmillan & Sons in 1957, and it was published under both of their names.

Strunk & White is succinct, clear, and comprehensive. It is, moreover, an enjoyable two-hour read, full of humor and lots of "aha!" moments. If you could have only one book on how to write, this would be that book.

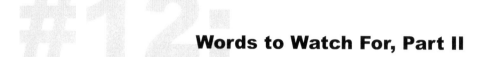

Words to Watch For, Part II

In *WordWorks* #7, we checked off a few of the words that give us all problems; here are some more. Thanks very much to those of you who nominated some of these.

Once again, the idea here is to become alert to these words when they show up in your writing—even if it's only to be sure you have used them correctly.

Its and It's

I make this correction in my own writing at least once a week. But, as we all know—but tend to overlook when we're typing rapidly—in this case the possessive ("its") has no apostrophe because the contraction ("it's" for "it is") requires one.
"Some people believe that **it's** the role of government to look after **its** citizens."

Amount and Number

Usually what happens is that we unthinkingly use "amount" when we really mean "number"; it rarely happens the other way around. Use "amount" when you refer to something that must be weighed or measured; use "number" when you refer to something you count.

Wrong: "The **amount** of students who vote using absentee ballots is surprisingly small."

Right "The **number** of students who vote using absentee ballots is surprisingly small."

Less and **Fewer**

This pair follows exactly the same rule: use "less" when you weigh or measure; use "fewer" when you count.

Wrong: "The ferry had **less** passengers than the captain expected."

Right: "The ferry had **fewer** passengers than the captain expected."

Affect and **Effect**

This pair makes it on to the list of frequently misused words for a couple of reasons. First of all, lots of folks confuse "affect" (the verb) with "effect" (the noun).

"He hopes that the new legislation will positively **affect** all of his constituents and that the main **effect** will be higher employment."

The other reason this pair is problematic is that each word (in spelling, at least) is also a whole other word. So, we have "affect", a noun, pronounced with a short "a", which has to do with expression or outward appearance.

"His paralysis meant that his face was without **affect**." "Her black turtleneck and beret conveyed a Bohemian **affect**."

"Effect", with a long initial "e", is a verb that means "to make happen", most often used with "change".

"Her only objective was to **effect** some sort of change in the organization."

#13:

Those Pesky Commas, Part II

Commas cause more trouble than all of the other punctuation marks put together. They are forever turning up in unexpected places and confusing things. This week we'll have another look at those troublesome little curves.

When we read, whether or not we read aloud, we "hear" the words, sentences, and paragraphs. Indeed, one of the characteristics of great writing is the beauty of what we might call the melody produced by the words. The job of punctuation is to provide a guide to the reader about how the words are supposed to "sound".

When we come across a period, we know that the sound of the final syllable is lowered; that's all there is to that. A question mark in that position tells us that the voice goes up, right?

The comma tells the reader to "Pause, something more is on its way." In many cases it also says that something is being inserted, just for enlightenment, not to change the basic idea of the sentence.

So:

"The Republican Party captured a majority of seats in Congress."

"The Republican Party, capitalizing on the sour mood of the independent voter, captured a majority of seats in Congress."

The piece between the commas comments on, but does not change, the sentence.

On the other hand:

"People who live in glass houses shouldn't throw stones."

This sentence says that *only* those living in glass houses should refrain from stonethrowing; for the rest of us it's not a problem.

Another way this works is in Direct Address.

In this sentence, "The police arrested my cousin, Bill." I am telling somebody called "Bill" about my unfortunate cousin. Without the comma, my cousin Bill is off to the hoosegow.

It also should be said that in many of these situations, the commas are largely a matter of the writer's choice. This is especially true with words like "however" and "therefore", when the interruption to the sentence is minor. One thing, though: if you use one comma, you must not, under any circumstances [comma goes here] forget the second one.

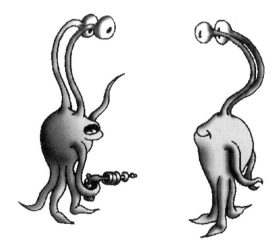

Let's go find their
leader, Gary.

#14: By the Numbers . . .

Often, especially when writing about research, numbers play an important role in what we wish to say. Like most other grammar considerations, the guiding principles in writing numbers are consistency and clarity. Reliably, the APA does present some guidelines, but even following those, you will find that you will need to make some judgment calls now and then.

1. The most basic APA guideline is to use numerals for all numbers 10 and higher. The major exception to this rule is that a sentence can't begin with a numeral.

   "Seventeen of the 21 students in the class arrived late for the lecture."

2. Another exception occurs when it is necessary to be consistent within a category.

   "She expected nine guests for dinner, so she made 10 individual pizzas, 3 of which were meatless." (Note: guests and pizzas are different categories. Also, the numbers of pizzas could just as well have been stated in words. But it would be incorrect to write, " . . . she made 10 individual pizzas, three of which were meatless." It is important to be consistent.

3. To indicate time, use numerals with A.M. or P.M. (6:30 A.M.); without A.M. or P.M., use words (six-thirty, eleven o'clock).

4. Use hyphens when you: spell out numbers between twenty-one and ninety-nine; spell out simple fractions (two-thirds, four-fifths); or combine numbers and words to make modifiers (10-point scale). (Note: if you had a bunch of 10-point scales, to avoid confusion you would spell out the quantity—fifteen 10-point scales.)

5. To write plural numbers, simply add an "s"-with no apostrophe.

"sixes and sevens" "10s and 20s"

"American culture underwent a profound dislocation during the 1960s and 1970s."

(Note: these decades could have been expressed as "the '60s and '70s" or as "the sixties and seventies"—your choice.)

These are some of the general basics. *The Publication Manual of the American Psychological Association* provides lots more detail, with especially useful information about writing numbers in statistics and results of experiments.

Ted was very impressed with
version 2.0 of his software package.

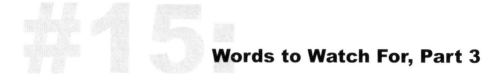

Words to Watch For, Part 3

It is difficult to imagine anything quite as confusing as the English language: it is constantly changing; what is perfectly acceptable in conversation is anathema in formal writing; and so many words sound a lot like other words.

Here are a few more words to add to the list of those we need to keep a careful eye on when revising. Thanks again to those who suggested these particular words.

Bring and Take

Your choice here depends on nothing more complicated than point of origin. If it's from *there* to *here*, choose "bring".

"'Be sure to bring your textbook to each class,' said the instructor."

But if it's from *here* to *there,* "take" is the word you want.

"Please take some of this cake home to your kids; I can't possibly eat it all."

This does get a little tricky with certain regional usage: in New York City and its suburbs, for example, they tend to "bring" everything everywhere, regardless. (They also stand "on" line rather than "in" line. Go figure.)

Accept and **Except**

We all *accept* that these two words have almost nothing in common, *except* that they sort of sound alike.

"Accept" means to receive without protest.

"The students accept their instructor's criticism."

"Except" means "leaving out".

"Every Senator except one voted in favor of the bill."

Continual and **Continuous**

"Continuous" means without interruption.

"His continuous bragging left everyone feeling somewhat annoyed."

"Continual" means over and over and over again.

"Her car's continual stalling made it pretty clear that a trip to the mechanic was unavoidable."

#16: Not Quite Dead

I've heard a question or two lately about "i.e." and "e.g." I hope this helps to clear things up.

For a long time now, we've been accustomed to referring to Latin—the language of the Roman Empire—as a "dead" language. It is true that the Catholic Church held on to Latin for its liturgies, but even that came to a halt (in our hemisphere at any rate) thirty-some years ago. So Latin is no longer a language of literature, business, politics, or conversation; but it has held on for certain ceremonial uses (some diplomas and ecclesiastical documents, for example). And it's right there on our money: "*E Pluribus Unum.*"

It also shows up in our everyday writing. And contractions of Latin expressions especially can give us trouble. But, actually, most if not all of that trouble can be avoided if we simply remember what the Latin expressions mean.

I.e.

"I.e." is a contraction for the Latin phrase *id est.*, which means "that is." We use it when we wish to clarify a generalization or abstraction by stating exactly what we mean.
 "He owns several automobiles, but usually drives his favorite one, i.e., his '64 Mustang."

E.g.

"E.g." is also a contraction of two Latin words, *exempli gratia*, literally "for the sake of an example;" we simplify it to mean "for example."

So:

"Only well-funded national newspapers, e.g., *The New York Times* and *The Wall Street Journal*, are likely to survive for very long in the digital age."

Etc.

Two Latin words, *et* (and) and *cetera* (other things), are contracted to make "etc.," which we use to save our reader the trouble of reading a long series of obvious items.

Once in a while, you will read a series that goes, "x, y, z, and etc." The "and" is obviously redundant. Remembering that "et" means "and" will take care of that.

More serious, however, is using "etc." to make your reader work too hard.

In this sentence, for example,

"We took out a second mortgage to repave the driveway, put in a brick sidewalk, plant ornamental trees, build a gazebo, etc."

 it is clear how the series might have continued.

But it would not be fair to your reader to write,

"We took out a second mortgage to repave the driveway, etc."

leaving him or her to figure out what else you might have done with the cash.

#17: One Way to Write an Introduction

As readers, we humans don't like not knowing where we are. We don't appreciate a discussion that begins in the middle. And we especially have a hard time when we lack a context. That's why an Introduction is so important.

The word itself tells us a lot about the job of the Introduction. It is formed from two Latin words: *intro-* "inward, to the inside" + *ducere* "to lead". "To lead (the reader from outside the piece of writing) to the inside," then, is what the Introduction needs to do.

There are many, many ways to do this, certainly. But one method that works well for virtually any piece of writing is to progress from a very broad generalization to a quite precise Thesis Statement.

An example.

Let's say that our thesis is something like: "Taking courses online is an attractive option because you can work when you want to, work from home, and get the undivided attention of the instructor." We'll put that at the end of our Introduction.

The first sentence needs to be a broad generalization, an attention-getter, and it also needs to define the context of the essay.

Something like:

"It is impossible to overstate the impact of technology on our lives over the past 20 years."

The next sentence would then be narrower in focus, something like: "From movies and music to coffee and cookies, we can get what we want faster and easier."

Then, even narrower: "One area in which the change has been most profoundly felt is in higher education."

And still narrower: "Hundreds of thousands of people have found that going to college online removes significant barriers that had previously stood in their way."

So our Introduction would go something like this:

"It is impossible to overstate the impact of technology on our lives over the past 20 years. From movies and music to coffee and cookies, we can get what we want faster and easier. One area in which the change has been most profoundly felt is higher education. Hundreds of thousands of people have found that going to college online removes significant barriers that had previously stood in their way. Clearly, taking courses online is an attractive option because you can work when you want to, work from home, and get the undivided attention of the instructor."

It's pretty easy to imagine the essay that would follow, and that's exactly the point. The Introduction should lead the reader into the essay so that what follows is no surprise.

Again, this is only one of many methods of constructing an Introduction. The method you choose is, of course, up to you. The main thing to keep in mind is that, as the writer, it is your job to LEAD your reader into your writing.

#18:

Writing and Speaking, Time and Space

Writing and speaking have a lot in common. We use both forms of communication to get business done, to persuade others to agree with our points of view, to amuse and entertain. Thinking about the ways they differ, though, can help us be better writers.

The essential difference between writing and speaking is that writing—like painting and sculpture—exists *only* in space, while speaking—like music—exists only in time. We can stop reading whenever we please and resume tomorrow or next week; we can go back and reread; we can see what we read right there on the page (or Kindle, if you like). Listening to a speaker, though, we get it the first time through or not at all.

Keeping this difference in mind when we write can help our writing in some trivial and not-so-trivial ways. Here are some of them:

<u>Repetition</u>

Good speakers understand that they must repeat important ideas if they expect their audiences to remember them. But in writing, too much repetition quickly grows irksome. As a reader, you think, "Yeah, got that. You don't need to keep saying it."

NOTE: when referring to a point you already made in a speech, use "before". ("As I mentioned before, . . . ") In writing, however, use "above". ("As noted above, . . . ")

<u>Conclusion</u>

Few words are as welcome to the audience at a long speech as, "In conclusion." They let us know that we're in the home stretch; soon we'll be standing up, heading for the rest room, and off homeward.
 In an essay, however, there's no need for those words at all. The reader can see right there on the page that we're nearly done, that this is the last section.

Furthermore, while a summing up may be absolutely necessary (see "Repetition" above) in the conclusion of a speech, it is almost always to be avoided in writing. Unless the piece of writing is extremely long (hundreds of pages), summarizing serves only to annoy the reader. ("Didn't I just read that two pages ago?") It's much better to use the conclusion to restate your thesis and bring things to a graceful close by returning to a point you made in your Introduction.

Say it simply; simply say it.

This week we'll take a look at a few words that just seem to overcomplicate our writing without adding anything at all.

Some words and phrases have come to sound somehow "official" to us. We hear them so often that we use them ourselves when we write. But many of those words do nothing to enhance what we are trying to say; indeed they get in the way.

For example:

<u>Utilize</u>

Here's a word that ought never be employed. Its synonym, "use" is always a better choice. The same goes for the related "utilization". Best to choose "use" instead. Don't worry. "Use" is a resilient little word. Not much risk of its wearing out from overutilization.

Then there are the phrases we could do without:

Do not write:	**Instead, do write:**
at a price of $9	$9
make an adjustment to	adjust
make an examination of	examine
make mention of	mention
make out a list	list
to the fullest possible extent	fully
are found to be in agreement	agree
it has been brought to my attention	I have learned

There are many, many more of these, of course. And you can find them in a book mentioned in an earlier *WordWorks: Writing for Results in Business, Government, The Sciences, and The Professions*, by David Ewing.

#20: Proofreading

Sometimes the hardest thing to do with a piece of writing is to go back and read it again. You want to be finished, already! But that extra effort is worth it—every time.

When you receive a letter or an email (We'll leave texts and tweets out of this discussion.) and misspellings and typos make it clear that the writer didn't bother to proofread before sending, the message you receive goes beyond what the writer may have wished to say.

Those kind souls among us will allow that the writer was just in a hurry, but the more critical reader will surely take offense. Not bothering to proofread says to the reader, "You're not worth the trouble."

That's probably not the message you'd like to send to your instructor.

So . . . some thoughts on proofreading:

Experiment with different proofreading methods.
Some people can very successfully read their work, find errors, and fix them right on the computer screen. Others of us have more success making corrections on paper. Find out which one works best for you.

Read your work out loud.
Proofreading is not easy, especially proofreading your own work. You know what you meant to say, and often that's what you will read—even if that's not what you wrote. Reading aloud will help you to hear what's actually there. Getting someone you trust to read to you is even more effective. If something sounds "not quite right" to you, it probably means you have some editing to do.

The most likely place for a typo is in a heading or title.

Our tendency is to read the "small print" (references, citations, etc.) much more closely than we read headings. So make sure you give them an extra look before you hit "send" or "print".

Get as much distance as you can.

When you are confident you have finished proofreading and everything is perfect, put your work away for awhile (an hour, a day, a couple of days-the longer, the better). Then come back and proofread again. You certainly will find something that needs fixing.

Due to an unfortunate typo, the new model had to be recalled to replace the hairbags.

#21:

What's the "it"?

Some people are just fascinated by technical jargon. They want to know the precisely correct names for things. The nurses among us, for example, know that guy's not just limping; no, he's suffering from "Claudication" (*limping caused by a reduction in blood supply to the legs*). Some enjoy sesquipedalian obscurantism (hiding the ordinary behind big words). For them it's not "water"; it's "dihydrogen monoxide".

So this week—for you jargonists—we're having a look at what are called, technically, "dangling participles".

But what they are called is not that important; we recognize them by what they *don't* tell us. Here's a pretty common example:

"By analyzing all the experimental data, **it** tells us that more than 50% of Americans do not see any reason to vote."

The question is, of course: What's the "it"? You can't know, because the "it" doesn't refer to anything. What the writer ought to have written was:

"Analyzing all the experimental data tells us that more than 50% of Americans do not see any reason to vote."

Simple fix, eh?

Another place this phantom "it" turns up is when the writer is discussing a book or article. Like this:

"In *Lady Chatterley's Lover* by D. H. Lawrence, it has a lot to say about hypocrisy."

What's the "it"?

Same fix:

"*Lady Chatterley's Lover* by D. H. Lawrence has a lot to say about hypocrisy."

Or, if the writer is talking more about the author, less about the book:

"In *Lady Chatterley's Lover* D. H. Lawrence has a lot to say about hypocrisy."

Either way, the reader knows, clearly, who it is that has a lot to say.

#22:
3 . . . 2 . . . 1 . . . Action!

By far the most important word in any sentence is the verb. (Indeed, a single verb can be a sentence: Fetch. Retreat. Go.) So it's worth spending an extra minute to try to come up with a better verb than the one we originally wrote.

A good place to start discriminating between verbs is to recall the two different kinds: action and being. When we write using "action" verbs, the subject DOES something. But when we use "being" verbs the subject IS; it exists. And, to a reader, action is always more interesting than being. Action verbs have more impact, are more easily understood, and are much more memorable.

The "being" verbs are the various forms of "to be": is, are, was, were, will be, etc. But they also include words like "appear" and "seem".

Obviously, you can't write in English without "being" verbs, so the idea is to find these and replace as many of them as possible with action verbs. Quite often, you'll find the action verb you want already lurking in the sentence, thus:

"She found his behavior to be appalling."

"His behavior appalled her."

Or . . .

"The faculty appointment is dependent upon sufficient enrollment."

"The faculty appointment depends upon enrolling enough students."

(Notice that sometimes one change leads to another. In the second example, not only is "depends" more interesting than "is dependent upon", but also "enrolling enough students" is more interesting than "sufficient enrollment".)

One more . . .

"Our society is over-reliant on automobiles and trucks for its transportation needs."

"Our society relies far too much on automobiles and trucks for its transportation needs."

Practice this by taking a paragraph that you have written and replacing all the being verbs with action ones.

(You'll also usually find that you use fewer words to make your point; always a good thing.)

#23: Who's On First?

Pronouns—words that take the place of nouns—can be tough to manage. They are a big topic, but let's make a start.

"Relative" pronouns are the ones we use to ask questions or to categorize nouns. Their inherent vagueness makes them incredibly useful and potentially confusing.

"Who" is one of these words, as the famous Abbott & Costello "Who's on first" routine illustrates. (Check it out on YouTube; it's still funny.)

So:

Who or **Whom**?
The technical answer to this question is that "who" is in the nominative case, and "whom" is in the objective case.

And what that means is that when the word is the doer of the action or describes the doer, use "who".

"Who wants to know?"

"Are you the thief who stole my iPad?"

And when the word is the recipient of the action, use "whom".

"I can't figure out whom to call."

"Who's insulting whom?"

"To whom it may concern . . ."

Who or **That**?

The answer to this dilemma is often a judgment call. But, in general, it just makes sense to use "who" when you are talking about people (especially specific people), and "that" when not.

"Parents who opt to home school their children have a long list of challenges to overcome."

"Samuel Johnson, who compiled the first English dictionary, was famous for his punning ability."

"The committee decided to discuss only those matters that could be dealt with on the spot."

But what about animals? Fluffy is a "who", not a "that", surely! The simple answer is the best: if the animal has a name, it's "who"; if not, it's "that".

"The bison that had been so diminished by wanton hunting are slowly gaining in numbers."

"She brought her cat, who yowled continuously, into the vet's examination room."

Inverted Commas

We Americans call them "quotation marks", but the English call them "inverted commas". Either way, they can be a little troublesome.

All of the schools in my town have recently been displaying a banner that reads: "We Make A Difference"—quotation marks included. Why have they quoted these words? Who said them? Or are the school administrators being sarcastic and suggesting that they actually don't make a difference. Surely not!

So what about quotation marks, anyway?

When we write we use them in several ways.

Firstly, and most obviously, we use them to designate words that someone actually said or wrote.

In his inaugural address in 1961, President John F. Kennedy famously said, "Ask not what your country can do for you; ask what you can do for your country."

Edgar Allen Poe's most famous poem, "The Raven", begins, "Once upon a midnight dreary, while I pondered, weak and weary . . ."

Secondly, as in the example above, we use them to indicate titles of short works, or works—poems, articles, chapters, songs—that can be found within larger works. The titles of larger works—collections, journals, novels, CDs—we put in italics.

"The Flaw in the Plan" is Chapter Thirty-Six of *Harry Potter and the Deathly Hallows* by J.K. Rowling.

Thirdly, we use quotation marks to indicate that we are pointing to a word as a word, rather than the thing it signifies.

The term "liberal" has changed its meaning over the last fifty years.

It is NOT a good idea to use quotation marks to underscore sarcasm or to imply disbelief. (This is the written equivalent of "air quotes".)

Her assistant was "working from home" that day and couldn't be reached.

The message here is extremely unclear, implying—but not saying out-right mistrust and censure. (It's pretty generally a bad idea to put sarcasm into writing at all, as it tends to come across as bitterness or scorn. If you don't like something, say that.)

#25: Words to Watch For, Part 4

Some time ago, an insurance company ran a series of television commercials that featured suggestions on how to stay healthy. One of these showed a woman parking her car at the extreme edge of the parking lot and walking from there to her office door. The words across the bottom of the screen read, "Health tip #17 (or whatever it was): Park Further Away."

Wrong.

Further means "more" or "additional," as in:

"With no further discussion, the legislature voted on the bill."

Farther has to do with distance; it is the opposite of "nearer".

"I was surprised at how much farther I could run in my new shoes."

(Note: After about six months, the commercial was corrected.)

Here's one that's beginning to gain in frequency: using **to** when **too** is called for.

"Too" means, of course, "also".

"He thought he'd like a milkshake too."

But it's also used to modify certain adjectives, meaning "excessively".

"Too many" "Too fat" "Too slow" "Too late"

(NOT "To many" etc.)

Not necessarily wrong, but . . .

"Oftentimes" is, if you think about it, redundant. I.e., the concept "often" is already about "time".

But if you decide to use it, **BE SURE** to write it as one word, "oftentimes"; "often times" is wrong.

Amongst in American English is an archaism.

It belongs here:

"I wouldst fain include thee amongst my cronies."

But we probably wouldn't write that way; we'd write something like:

"I'd like to have you among my friends."

Subheads

It always feels good when, unexpectedly, the GPS lady interrupts your conversation to give you her next directional update. "Exit to the right in 2.6 miles," lets you know where you are and what will happen next. You know you are approaching the exit, and you know that you're ending this phase of the journey to begin a new one.

Your readers will feel the same way when you use subheads to let them know where they are in your paper, article, essay, letter, report, or proposal. Just as it's a great idea to spend some time coming up with a title for your writing that captures what's inside, it's also worth the trouble to devise subheads that engage, inform, and provide direction.

Ask Questions

One way to write subheads is to ask the question the following section is intended to answer. This strategy can be particularly useful in laying out a case or making a proposal:

What is The Problem?

What is The Proposed Solution?

Who Will Implement The Solution?

What Is The Plan of Work?

How Much Will It Cost?

Get Functional

Reports and plans have some tried and true subheads. Everybody knows what to expect when they see:

Background

Objectives

Literature Review

Target Audience

Desired Outcomes

Stay Focused

Lots of ASAP writing assignments involve applying academic learning to personal or business or professional experiences of the student. The trick here is always to let the reader know when you're about to switch.

That could be a simple as:

Theory 1

Practice 1

Theory 2

Practice 2

And so forth.

Or you might consider naming names:

MacGillicuddy's Best Practices

Early Sunday Morning, The Crouse Hospital ER

#27:

P. O. V.

You have probably heard by now something like, "Don't use 'I' when you write." Or "Use the third person." What we're really telling you is to consider the point of view you wish to use in writing. And there's more to it than you might think.

In the Friday February 25, 2011 New York Times, columnist David Brooks wrote, "The country also needs a substantive debate about the role of government." Notice that he didn't begin his remark with "I believe" or "I think", even though what he is clearly up to is expressing his own opinion.

What Brooks is doing is writing "objectively" or writing "in the third person," and that's exactly the point of view students should adopt in nearly all of the writing you do for your courses.

One of the things over which you have control when you write is this "point of view". You have three from which to choose: first person, "I or we"; second person "you" (as in this paragraph), and third person "he, she, or it".

Clearly, when you are writing an "Autobiography" or "My Life Journey"—as many of you have—it would be kind of silly to write in the third person. You are writing about yourself, so the first person is entirely appropriate. The same goes for certain more informal reaction or reflection essays.

The customary point of view for most academic writing, however, is the third person, because it allows you to take yourself out of the equation, to be more objective.

When you are writing a position paper, for example, using the first person will tend to weaken your argument, sending the message: "It's only my opinion, but . . . "

Instead, follow Mr. Brooks' lead and state your opinion as an objective fact. You don't need to say, "I learned (or I believe, or I think, etc.) that the deficit must be solved." State it as a fact, **even if it's an opinion.** "The deficit must be solved."

In a research paper, use the first person to report what you did or will do. "In my research, I will survey 65 employees."

Or, you could simply describe the situation: "Step two of the research will entail surveying 65 employees."

Another option—less graceful—is to use the passive voice: "65 employees will be surveyed."

What you really DON'T want to do is use the "this writer believes" or "the researcher will survey" dodge. Those are simply first-person point of view written without using "I".

(And keep alert for examples of the scholarly/academic "objective" point of view. As you consult journals and other periodicals in your research, you'll find many. Check out how the pros do it.)

#28:

The Apostrophe

A new restaurant recently opened in our area, and we were interested in finding out about it. So, naturally, straight to Google we went. We found the website for the place, but quickly decided that we wouldn't become patrons. One of the specialties of the house, apparently, is many varieties of burgers. And right there, prominently displayed on the restaurant's menu, appeared the heading:

"Burger's".

I am sure the proprietors meant "Burgers".

Possession

Nearly all English words indicate possession with an apostrophe.

When they are singular, they also add an "s"—even when they end in "s":

Toyota's image problem   The house's color scheme   James's guitar

When plural, no added "s":

His clients' reputations   Patients' meals   Her friends' iPhones

(Note: in the plural possessive, the things possessed are plural too. Wouldn't be much fun if everybody had to share one iPhone.)

Of course, there are exceptions:

Certain ancient proper names that end in " s" do not need another after the apostrophe.

So: Moses' followers, Osiris' statue, Jesus' teachings. (The truth is that we would probably not usually use this form, preferring instead: "The followers of Moses", "the statue of Osiris", etc.)**

Pesky Pronouns

Hers, its, theirs, yours, and ours—all possessive—do not use the apostrophe. But other pronouns (called "indefinite pronouns") do: "It's important to make one's opinion heard." or "I think I took someone else's raincoat by mistake."

Quotes in Quotes

The other common use of the apostrophe is to minimize confusion when a quoted passage contains a quote.

The Professor insisted, "The opening sentence of Moby Dick, 'Call me Ishmael,' is one of the finest sentences ever written."

**Strunk, W., & White, E. (2000). The Elements of Style (4th ed., p. 1). New York, NY: Longman.

Words to Watch For, Part V

Filler Words:

Certain words seem to find their way into our writing, even though they don't add very much, if anything, to what we are trying to communicate.

In a previous *WordWorks,* for example, we talked about beginning a final paragraph with the words "in conclusion", never mind that the reader can clearly see the end of the essay coming right up.

Think of these words as filler.

Another perennial "filler word" is **truly.**

To be sure, "truly" is a perfectly useful word in some circumstances- when it means the opposite of "falsely".

So, it's perfectly fine to write:

"Bob cleared his throat loudly a few times to make sure she was truly asleep."

But, expressions like "I truly believe . . . " and "We truly care . . . ", are no different meaningwise from "I believe . . ." and "We care . . .".

In these cases **truly** is simply filler. Leave it out.

Compounds:

Overtime means something different from **over time.**

If something is said to happen "over time" it will take awhile.

"Overtime", on the other hand, is almost always used with the idea of work. You are working "overtime" when you're putting in more time on the job than you had planned or agreed to. (This could be a very good thing if your union contract gets you time and a half for it.)

Similarly, **anymore** and **any more** have very different meanings.

"Any more" usually refers to quantity.

"You can't have any more until you finish what's on your plate."

"Anymore" is a time word.

"You can't do that anymore."

#30: Parallel Structure

"A foolish consistency is the hobgoblin of little minds, adored by little statesmen and philosophers and divines."
—Ralph Waldo Emerson**

We can all find inspiration in Emerson's declaration. Just because we thought a thing yesterday doesn't mean we must continue to think it all our lives.

But, if we wish to be understood, consistency in writing is of another kind, and it is crucial. Indeed, much of what we learned as "grammar" is, if you think about it, nothing more than making sure we express ourselves consistently.

We need, in sentences, to make sure that when the subject is singular so is the verb. And at the sentence or paragraph level, we need to choose a tense in which to write (usually present or past) and a point of view (typically the objective third person or the personal first person) and stick with it.

Parallel Structure

Consistency applies to series or lists, too. And this can get a little complicated. The fundamental necessity is the same, though.

So:

In this list, item 4 is inconsistent with the others-
  1. deciding whom to include and whom to exclude
  2. arranging for travel to and from the airport
  3. choosing menu items for all meals
  4. reimburse employees for out of pocket expense
  5. cleaning the area

All but #4 are "ing" words (nouns, actually-well, gerunds if you want to be technical); #4 is a verb. Parallel structure (consistency) demands that they all be the same.

Same thing applies when the "list" is not stacked or numbered:

"The successful leader will take pains to evaluate all options, gain buy-in from the team, forceful action, keep the dream alive, and learn from mistakes."

"Forceful action", however much we might admire it, is a noun among verbs, and thus doesn't belong here; insert "take" in front of it to make all well.

That's all there is to parallel structure: whatever the items are (noun, verb, command, question, sentence, whatever), they all need to be the same. They need to be consistent—though, of course, not foolishly so.

**Atkinson, B. (Ed.). (1968). The selected writings of Ralph Waldo Emerson (p. 152). New York, NY: The Modern Library.

#31.
Thinking About
Writing About Research

Some of the papers you'll be asked to write in your ASAP program will require that you use research to support your thesis. A few things to keep in mind about using research include:

—The whole idea behind researching a topic is that you become an expert in whatever it is that you're writing about and therefore that what you write is taken seriously.

—Use research not just to support your thesis, but to help you figure out just what your thesis is in the first place. A quick review of journal articles can let you know what kinds of things experts are saying about your topic. Reacting to what somebody else has written is a great way to come up with a thesis.

—When you begin your research, it's a good idea to use the broadest search term you can. You'll get lots of articles to look through, but just by scanning the titles you'll begin to get a feel for the field. You can narrow your searches later on when you have a tighter definition of what your topic really is.

—Make sure you take notes at every step of the research journey. Especially on a very large project (an Action Research Project, for example), detailed notes can save you from having to go back and re-research important sources. Also: it can be very useful to include in your notes your own thoughts on, reactions to, and opinions about the article/book/website you are consulting. You will find these "notes to self" to be valuable assets when you actually sit down to write.

—Beware of overusing research in the writing of your paper. A collection of quotes cannot, in any sensible way, be called "writing." In other words, the bulk of your paper should be your own ideas and words; use research to support or to provide evidence for your own points and claims.

Had historians dug a little deeper,
they would have realized Napoleon wasn't short.
He was simply experimenting with trench warfare.

#32: Order!

Sometimes the fundamentals of good writing are just versions of the skills we need to navigate the world at large. Humans are pretty much hard wired to abhor chaos, so putting things in order is an important skill to master.

"Order" is a very interesting word, one with many meanings.

When you tell your server what you would like for lunch, we say you "order". The instructions that the young lieutenant gives to her platoon will be more likely carried out if she adds, "that's an order." When the judge calls for "order in the court," he wants everybody to shut up and behave. In biology, an "order" is a group of several families of organisms. This list could go on. (Indeed, if you Google the word, you'll find something approaching 60 definitions.)

What they all have in common is that "order" is always a quality that helps us make sense of the world. As readers, we need order to understand what we are reading; so as writers, it's up to us to provide that order—at all levels.

Organization

We need to put our remarks in an order that a reader might expect. Writing an autobiography, for example, we'd want to follow chronological order. Having told the story of my father's retirement party, I couldn't simply jump into a story of how he got a promotion—not, at least, without letting the reader know why I was jumping back in time.

Syntax

The order of words in a sentence can dramatically affect the meaning.

"For Sale: One maple table by elderly lady with chipped legs."

It's probably not the old lady whose legs are chipped, so . . .

"For Sale: One maple table with chipped legs by elderly lady."

Or

"There would be a baked good waiting for him or a cup of coffee."

The baked good isn't waiting for a cup of coffee, so . . .

"There would be a baked good or a cup of coffee waiting for him."

Where to put "only"

The word most often found in the wrong spot in a sentence is certainly "only". And it can make quite a difference, so take a minute to make sure it's in the right place.

A great writing teacher and old friend of mine, Henry Jankiewicz, came up with this fun exercise to keep us aware of the possibilities.

In this sentence,

"He said that he loved her."

You can place "only" in every location, thus:

"Only he said that he loved her." "He only said that he loved her." "He said only that he loved her." And so forth.

Each location of "only" changes the sentence's meaning.

#33: More Reading about Writing

Searching the "Books" section of Amazon.com for "Writing Skills" yields no fewer than 96 titles. And that, I'm sure, only scratches the surface. There are hundreds more writing books from which to choose, and they all no doubt have some value.

I'd like to share a few books that I can recommend as being particularly useful for writing, both in an academic setting and on the job. (By the way, I did a quick check, and all three of these are available on Amazon . . . Used!)

1. *Everything's an Argument,* by Andrea A. Lunsford and John J. Ruszkiewicz

This is one of those books that is a kind of one-stop shop for student writers. And it would be a terrific book if that's all it was. But its great virtue is suggested by the title. It is extremely useful for a writer to keep in mind that ALL writing is, at some level, an attempt to persuade the reader to agree.

(If you are writing a Literature Review for your Action Research Project, you are making a de facto case that your research is an important addition to the field. In a Book Report you aim to convince the reader that your take on the book is the right one. The writer of meeting minutes gets to "officially" define what happened there.)

The book does a good job of dissecting arguments, figuring out what works and what doesn't, and understanding what kind of persuasion and evidence to use depending on the objective.

2. *The Practical Stylist* by Sheridan Baker

Of course there are lots of ways to write an essay, but Baker's book presents a kind of formula—the "keyhole"—that is comprehensible, adaptable, easy-to-learn, and—best of all—always works.

This book has been around for many years, and of all the writing texts there are, it is one of the very best for self study. I have often recommended it to students who wanted to work on their own to improve their writing, and I have never known it to fail.

3. *The Copywriter's Handbook* by Robert W. Bly

The subtitle tells the story: "A Step-By-Step Guide to Writing Copy That Sells." And while this may seem at first to have little application to academic or other kinds of professional writing, in fact the skills employed by advertising writers are essentially the same as those we all need to keep in mind when we write: the purpose of writing is to communicate; know your audience; know your subject; get the reader's attention. As an advertising writer himself, Bly practices what he preaches; so this book is a lot of fun to read, even if you couldn't care less about advertising!

#34: Think Small

An iconic magazine ad for the Volkswagen Beetle shows a tiny car in the upper left hand corner of an all-white page. At the bottom of the page is the headline, "Think Small." The idea that something so small could deliver big benefits was exactly tuned to counteract the conspicuous consumption represented by the gas guzzling behemoths coming out of Detroit back then. They sold a lot of VWs.

Generally speaking, the simpler and more direct you can make your writing, the better it will be. There is real power in brevity. That observation extends to words, too.

Two-letter words, in fact, can carry quite a load of meaning, more than you might imagine for such little things. They can also make our writing crisper and more interesting to read.

(By the way, I was astonished to learn that "Aa", "Jo", "Ka", and "Ta" are legal Scrabble words. Who knew?)

So

This little word can do a lot of work, making it clear that one thing follows from another. For example, when you've finished quoting or referring to a source in a research paper, start the next sentence with "so" to make it clear you're done with the source and are now drawing your own conclusions.

"The average American child spends more than 40 hours per week watching television" (Holmes & Watson, 2006, p. 18). So it's not that surprising that academic performance has been declining.

No

It is always clearer and more precise to make positive statements: expressing what is rather than what is not. "No" allows us to express negatives positively, as it were.

"He did not have any more patience with the situation."

"He had no more patience with the situation."

"Thomas Hardy did not write any novels after *Jude the Obscure.*"

"Thomas Hardy wrote no novels after *Jude the Obscure.*"

As

Expressing cause and effect can sometimes be tricky. Perhaps the simplest way is by using "as".

"As more than half of the class failed to show up, the instructor had no choice but to cancel."

(Beware of the colloquial "being that" or "being as"; they are conversational, but should never be used in formal writing. "As" does the job admirably.)

#35: Words to Watch For, Part VI

"Mnemonics" are little tricks that help us remember stuff. My piano teacher, for example, made me learn the lines and spaces of the Treble Clef: Every Good Boy Does Fine (EGBDF) were the notes represented by the lines, and FACE were those represented by the spaces. (It's still not clear to me that every good boy does indeed do fine, but, whatever . . .)

Similarly, most of us memorized the little rhyme ("Thirty days hath September . . . ") without which our calendar watches would be hopeless. And who didn't learn the alphabet as a song?

Principal/Principle

The nuns taught us the mnemonic for "principal": the princiPAL of the school is your "pal", so principal means the leader or the first in rank. (It can be a noun or an adjective.)

"He was fortunate to be promoted from principal to superintendent." (noun)

"Her principal reason for relocating was to be near her son." (adjective)

"Principle", the homonym, means fundamental law or belief or rule. (It can only be a noun.)

"The did their best to base the new online curriculum on sound pedagogical principles."

Advice/Advise

Using the right one of this pair also involves remembering which part of speech each one is. Simply: "advice" is a noun; "advise" is a verb.

When you give advice to your daughter, you advise her.

Comprise/Compose

The two words look at things from opposite points of view.

"Comprise" is essentially the equivalent of "embrace". While "compose" suggests "is an ingredient in" or "is part of".

So:

"The Center for Professional Studies at Keuka College comprises ASAP and International Programs."

But:

"ASAP and International Program compose the Keuka College CPS."

#36=
What Do You Mean By That?

Wordworks Quiz I

Certain words and expressions are so often used wrongly that what they really mean gets lost. Here's a little quiz involving some of those. Give yourself a star if you get all six right!

1. "Obviate" most nearly means . . .
   a.   Clarify
   b.   Make unnecessary
   c.   Make obvious
   d.   Destroy

2. To "beg the question" is to . . .
   a.   Ignore the ramifications
   b.   Describe a circumstance
        that requires a question
   c.   Prove an assertion by assuming
        the assertion is true
   d.   Forget to ask

3. "Disinterested" most nearly means . . .
   a.   Objective
   b.   Lazy
   c.   Left out of a will
   d.   Not interested

4. An "Abstract" is . . .
   a.   An Introduction
   b.   A Précis
   c.   An Executive Summary
   d.   An Outline

5. "Downfall" most nearly means . . .
    a. Failure
    b. Error
    c. Skydive
    d. Fatal Weakness

6. "Blatant" most nearly means . . .
    a. Noisily conspicuous
    b. Outstanding
    c. Brazen
    d. Singular

Albert had no idea how dangerous mixing metaphors could be until he tried to hoe a hard road.

Answers: 1. b.; 2. c.; 3. a.; 4. b.; 5. d.; 6. a.

#37: Problem Solving

In an effort to provide students with information they can use to make a difference right away in their writing, it's time to present the Top Ten most common student writing problems.

These are entirely my rankings; they have no scientific or statistical validity whatsoever. I have noted the prevalence of these problems in the hundreds and hundreds of papers and essays I have encountered, not only in my role as writing specialist for ASAP students, but also in more than thirty years as writing teacher and coach, both in and out of academe. I have a hunch that most writing teachers would agree, if not with the exact order of these items, at least with the things I've included.

The Top Ten

1.   Run ons
2.   Titles
3.   Introductions/Thesis Statements
4.   Conclusions
5.   Dangling Participles
6.   APA formatting basics
7.   Apostrophes
8.   Agreement
9.   Use of sources
10.   Proofreading for sense

Contrary to David Letterman's practice, I'm going to begin with Number One; we will get to the rest of the list in future *Wordworks*.

Number One: Run Ons

A sentence is a single idea. Some person or thing does something to some other person or thing. (Or some person or thing is whatever he/she/it is.)

"Run On" sentences happen when two ideas are joined together in a single sentence without sufficient notice to the reader. They are confusing.

"Listening is a skill **and** listening skills allow us to make sense of what other people are saying."

This probably the most common form of run on sentence. Two ideas, "Listening is a skill." and "Listening skills allow us to make sense of what other people are saying." are combined using the word "and".

The fix is simple: put a comma (and the "and") after the first idea.

So:

"Listening is a skill, and listening skills allow us to make sense of what other people are saying."

NOT

"Listening is a skill, listening skills allow us to make sense of what other people are saying." (You need the "and".)

OR

"Listening is a skill listening skills allow us to make sense of what other people are saying." (You need the comma and the "and".)

BUT YOU COULD, if you wanted to, use a **semicolon** instead of the , **and:**

"Listening is a skill; listening skills allow us to make sense of what other people are saying."

Another Example:

RUN ON

"For some folks, travel is a trip to Europe or to a far away lush resort and others consider travel a two-hour car ride to Mom's house."

FIXED

"For some folks, travel is a trip to Europe or to a far away lush resort, and others consider travel a two-hour car ride to Mom's house."

OR

"For some folks, travel is a trip to Europe or to a far away lush resort; others consider travel a two-hour car ride to Mom's house."

While Bob stayed up waiting for his daughter, to come home from her date, his eyes began to play tricks on him.

#38:

What's In A Title?

Number two on the Top Ten most common writing problems list is: overlooking the power of the title. Lots of essays and papers that come across my desk have titles like, "Leadership Paper" or "Auto-biography" or "Marketing Strategy".

These are certainly "titles", strictly speaking, but they stop way short of doing the kind of work for their writers that they could be doing.

That's because the title, right there on the front page of the assignment, is the first thing your reader encounters. And it's your golden opportunity not only to make a good first impression, but also to help your reader have a better idea about what's inside.

Newspapers have always known the power of the headline (their version of a title). Have a look any day at the home page of any major newspaper; you will see headlines whose job it is to help you decide (maybe even persuade you) about what you'll read.

On the May 31, 2011 NYTimes.com, for example, down near the bottom in the "Travel" section, we find: "On the Farm, After the Fall: Agritourism in the Former USSR." We have a pretty good idea what to expect in this article . . . certainly a better one than if it had been titled, "Travel Article."

As you see from the Times example, your title doesn't need to be especially clever to be effective. Some ways to come up with a good title include:

- Use a popular cliché or well known song lyric—a paper on the growth of Community College enrollments, for example, might be titled "Stairway to Heaven" or, perhaps, "Running With the Pack."

OR

- Read through the paper itself. I guarantee you will find a phrase that will make a good title.

OR

- Simply state the topic: "Community College Enrollment Growth."

In any of these options you might wish to follow the "catchy" title with a colon and a more explanatory phrase (as the Times headline writer did), thus:

"Stairway to Heaven: Growing Numbers of Adults Pursue Associates Degrees to Enhance Job Prospects."

The main thing is to **TITLE EVERYTHING,** and don't settle for generics. Try to find the title that could work ONLY with your wonderful paper!

#39:

Well Begun Is Half Done.

When you're writing those essays and papers that you have been as-signed, it can be easy to figure that what you're writing about is ob-vious; everybody in the class is doing the same assignment, after all. But even in those circumstances, each piece of writing must be able to stand on its own, and that means, in order to be successful, it must be-gin by introducing itself.

So you're at this party. Up steps a fellow with squinty eyes, a sallow complexion, and a knowing look. "I would urge caution," says he, "about speculative selling of deep in-the-money naked calls on any stock, expecting the stock price to plummet, as you would inevitably be exposing yourself to potentially unlimited losses."

You, naturally, run away, dialing the police as you go.

Had he, however, begun by introducing himself: "Hello, I'm Ed, and I'm a former investment banker, now working as a consumer advocate," you would at least understand that he meant well and that he was speaking in jargon.

Introductions are very, very important in writing, too. So they're number 3 on the Top Ten List.

Indeed, to your reader, beginning your essay with a discussion of the issue with no introduction is just as jarring and confusing as the encounter with Ed described above.

The function of the Introduction is threefold:

First, to let the reader know the subject, in general;

Second, to provide some sense of context (It makes a great deal of difference, for example, if you're discussing the 1964 Cadillac as a work of art or as a symbol of everything wrong with 20th-Century American culture.);

Third, to let the reader know why this discussion matters, what are the factors that led you to it.

Somewhere in the Introduction, usually near the end, you'll include your Thesis Statement, which will tell your reader quickly and clearly what to expect in the Body of the Essay that follows.

Wordworks #6 and #17 discussed "how-to" write an Introduction and Thesis Statement.

(Note: As you know, APA style calls for an Abstract. That's not to be confused with an Introduction. An Abstract is a very brief summary or précis of the entire essay.)

#40: All's Well That Ends Well.

When we experience music, art, writing, drama—or dinner, for that matter—we, as humans, need order and completeness to make sense of things. We like beginnings, middles, and ends.

We are discomfited when a song abruptly stops in the middle; we'd scratch our heads if the curtain came down just as Hamlet was dying.

As readers, especially, we really don't like it when the piece we are reading feels incomplete, when it feels like it stopped in the middle of things.

So Conclusions are number 4 on the Top Ten List. (Interestingly, one of Roget's synonyms for the word "conclusion" is "completion".)

In many ways, a good Conclusion is very like the mirror image of the Introduction.

Your Introduction establishes context, lets us know why we ought to be interested, and states your Thesis; so the Conclusion restates your thesis and, in effect, says, "There. Aren't you glad you read this? Don't you see how this all fits together?"

In a persuasive essay, you might go a bit further to suggest (though not in so many words) that, "the world would be a better place if everybody would just agree with me!"

We have observed elsewhere, but it bears repeating, that—especially in a relatively short piece of writing, of the length you'll produce for most of your courses—there is really no need to summarize. In fact, summarizing a short essay is pretty much guaranteed to annoy your reader. ("What the heck? Didn't I just read that?")

But even if, in a longer piece—an Action Research Project, for example—you do need to summarize, you still need to provide a conclusion after the Summary.

Likewise, in a short essay, you don't need to begin your conclusion with the words, "In conclusion." Your reader is looking at the page; he or she can see that you are nearing the end, that this is the final section.

Like most things about writing well, concluding your essay is really just paying attention to your reader. Make sure he or she goes away happy.

Refu geese.

#41:
Mysterious . . .

Pronouns (words like "it", "they", "their", and "which") by themselves are inherently vague. We need to work hard to make sure that our reader knows exactly who or what is being discussed.

Dangling participles are confusing precisely because of the mysterious pronoun problem, and they do make it hard for the reader to know what's what. So dangling participles (and other mysteries) are number 5 on the Top Ten list.

Here's one, for example:

"By analyzing the results, it will tell us what the next steps should be."

What is the "it"? To what does "it" refer? In fact, that word refers to nothing at all, and the sentence ought to read:

"Analyzing the results will tell us what the next steps should be."

(This turns up so often in our writing, I think, because we use it in conversation all the time. But that doesn't make it any less confusing when we read it.)

We very often dangle participles in relation to books or articles.

"In the *Publication Manual of the American Psychological Association, Sixth Edition,* it says that personal communication must be cited, but not included on the References page."

Once again: what's the "it"? Once again: nothing at all.
"*The Publication Manual of the American Psychological Association, Sixth Edition* says that personal communication must be cited, but not included on the References page."

Another maker of mysterious sentences is the Passive Voice (when the subject of the sentence receives rather than commits the action).

Thus, in a sentence like this:

"It is expected that the program overall will go according to schedule."

We have no idea what the "it" refers to; we can't know who is doing the expecting. It's a mystery.

"The Project Manager expects the program to go according to schedule."

Whether he or she likes it or not, that Program Manager is on record, and we know whom to blame (or credit).

#42:

Looking Good in Print
. . . APA Style

One of the challenges of writing in the workplace is making your document pleasing to the eye of the reader. Indeed, any writing—proposal, report, white paper, or college essay—makes an impression on the reader well before he or she actually reads any of the words.

Imagine that you are looking at two pages of printed text from ten or fifteen feet away. The page on the left is solid, single-spaced type, with no paragraph breaks. The page on the right is double-spaced, with headings, and paragraphs. Without knowing anything else about these pages, you would be more kindly disposed to the page on the right.

At work, it's up to you to make that document friendly and appealing. In your ASAP coursework, luckily, all you have to do is follow **APA style and formatting.** And, so, APA style is number six on the Top Ten List.

It is true that the APA is prescriptive about the minutest details and that rule changes from edition to edition of the manual can be frustrating. But for nearly all of the writing you will do for your courses, **following the General Format** will be mostly what you need to do. That means:

  --Everything is double-spaced
  --One-inch margins all around
  --10 - 12 pt. Times New Roman or Arial font
  --Title Page with Running Head in upper left and page 1 on upper
    right.
  --Following pages have Header on upper left and page number on
    upper right of every page.

Everything else you can (and should) look up, based on your specific needs.

APA format: it's no laughing matter.

#43:

Them Floating Comma Things

You may be interested to know that 2011 was the tenth anniversary of the founding of the <u>Apostrophe Protection Society.</u> You wouldn't think that harmless little "floating comma"** would need all that much protecting, would you?

I am convinced that nearly all student writers, if asked in the abstract how they should use an apostrophe, would pretty much know the right answers:

1. **To show possession:**

   Mike's falafel, the cat's meow, my laptop's performance, one's own work.

   (Except, of course, in the case of its, theirs, yours, and ours.)

2. **To show that letters are missing, that the word is a contraction:**

   "Can't" for cannot, "didn't" for did not, "won't" for will not (shouldn't it be "willn't"?) , etc.

And I am equally certain that those student writers would know that **plural words that are not possessive** DO NOT get an apostrophe.

BMWs (**not** "BMW's") are great cars. Cellphones (not "cellphone's") can't be used while driving in New York. The authors (**not** "author's") collaborated.

But some plural words are also possessive, and the apostrophe goes after the "s", thus:

Two weeks' notice, the ballplayers' union, patients' rights.

The problem is: even though we all know the right way to use apostrophes, we use them wrongly all the time. That's why they're (for "they are") number seven on the Top Ten list.

(NOTE: You can find more information on Apostrophes in *WordWorks* #28.)

**Truss, L. (2004). *Eats, shoots, and leaves*. Profile Books.

#44: Let's Agree to . . . Agree!

A consistent theme in the *Wordworks* series has been . . . consistency, how it makes it easier for our readers to understand what we write. Indeed, it's not too much to say that, though we can learn all sorts of grammatical dos and don'ts, what grammar really boils down to is being consistent.

It's important to be consistent in lots of ways: pick a tense (present or past) and stick with it; if a pronoun refers to a single person or thing, it ought to be singular; if you write a list, all of the items in the list should be the same kind of words (noun, verb, sentence, attribute, whatever).

But the problem that ranks number eight on the Top Ten list is consistency of *Number* between subject and verb, a.k.a. **Subject/Verb Agreement.** (In grammar, there are only two "Numbers": one thing-singular-or more than one-plural.)

"The number of the **subject** determines the number of the **verb**"*: i.e, if the subject is singular, the verb has to be singular, too.

— This is true even when there are lots of words in between.

"The real **pleasure** (subject) of college stud--dealing with ideas, making friends, challenging beliefs--**sticks** (verb) with us long after we graduate."

— A construction that often throws us off is "one of".

"Stephen Hawking is **one of** the most important scientists who **have (NOT "has")** ever lived." (It's the "scientists" who have lived.)

— On the other hand, "none" (meaning "not one") pretty much always gets a singular verb.

"None of the administrators **has** a clue."

"None of the dogs **was** housebroken."

— A subject is **plural** when several things are joined with the word "and".

"A fool **and** his money **are** soon parted."

"The novel **and** the movie that was made from it **capture** our hearts."

— But the subject remains **singular** when other items are added to it, using words such as "as well as", "with", and "in addition to".

"The sailboat **with** all of its accoutrements **fits** in my tiny garage."

"The President **as well as** the Secretary of State and the Speaker of the House **is** expected to address Congress.?

* Strunk, Jr., W., & White, E. (2000). *The Elements of Style* (4th ed., pp. 9-10). New York, NY: Longman.

Sources of Credibility

I am not one of those who in expressing opinions
confine themselves to facts.
—Mark Twain

If we're being honest, I suspect we'd all be guilty, along with Mr. Twain, of not necessarily basing our opinions solely on facts. But in writing for college, it's a good idea to try your best to do just that.

Why do research at all? Besides the obvious ("My instructor told me to."), the basic reason goes back to that core truth: we write to be read. And if our reader is to take us seriously, to pay attention to what we have to say, it's our job as writers to demonstrate that we know what we're talking about, that we are credible.

Especially in academe, credibility derives from displaying an awareness of what's already been written on our topic. That's where the research comes in.

Using the results of that research in our writing is number nine on the Top Ten List of common writing problems.

So here are just a few things to keep in mind when using sources in your research papers:

Introduce the source. Let the reader know that what is coming up is by someone other than you.

In the passage below, for example, the writer is referring to Jim Collins's valuable book, *Good to Great*. But that book has not been mentioned in the paper previously.

"This is not always possible, however, as discussed in Collins's book. A leader must figure out how to get the right people on the bus, move people on or off the bus, and seat people in the right seats who are already on the bus. The bus refers to the organization to which one belongs."

The reference to Collins here needs to be introduced. Something like:

"In *Good to Great* (2001), Jim Collins uses the metaphor of seats on the bus to describe the organizational challenge. A leader must figure out how to get the right people on the bus, move people on or off the bus, and seat people in the right seats who are already on the bus (p. XX)."

Fit your sentence to the quote. Since you didn't write it, you can't alter the source, so make your sentence fit it.

(My sentence) What we can say for sure about consumerism and the environment is that, (quoted passage) " . . . buying more and more unnecessary things is damaging our planet and contributing to global warming" (Sato, R., 2007, p. 136).

Keep it short. Especially using quotes, include only as much from the original as you need to make your point.

But make sure that, in doing so, you quote accurately. If, for example, you begin in mid sentence, or leave words out of a sentence, use an ellipsis (. . .) to indicate that there's more in the original than you have quoted.

If you didn't write it, you must cite it. Otherwise you will be guilty of plagiarism.

#46: That's Not What I Meant, At All!

Some of the most highly esteemed—though not necessarily highly paid—professionals in the publishing and advertising businesses are proofreaders. And the best of them are adept not only at finding mis-spellings, typos, and unfortunate grammar, but also at discriminating between sometimes very slight shades of meaning, making sure that the writing conveys exactly what it is meant to convey.

Those proofreaders are necessary because even professional writers are not all that great at proofreading their own work. Yet, as a student, that's precisely what you must try your best to do.

It's important enough that it ranks number **ten** on our list of writing problems.

Let's jump right in . . .

"The communicability of the disease has an estimated attack rate of 90% in household contacts developing the disease after exposure."

This sentence is confusing largely because it's so abstract. (Also, it's not the communicability, but the disease itself that has an attack rate, right?) How about:

"90% of people who are exposed to the disease at home contract it."

Sometimes a laudable impulse to state things unequivocally results in our going a little too far, forgetting about reality.

"Belief in life after death not only guarantees success in the hereafter, but also makes this world full of peace and happiness by making individuals responsible and dutiful in their activities."

A few "qualifiers" will do the trick here:

"Belief in life after death not only **helps us aspire to** success in the hereafter, but also **has the potential to** make this world full of peace and happiness by making individuals responsible and dutiful in their activities."

Sometimes stating a fact all by itself leaves the reader asking lots of questions.

"In the late 1950s nurse educators were identified as having prestigious education titles."

This is probably a factual statement. But why is it important that they were **"identified"**? And, by the way, was this **all, some,** or **just a few** nurse educators? Was this **big news** or **status quo**?

Then, finally, there's the ubiquitous "they".

"My opinion is that the nation's crime reports are as accurate as **they** can make them to be."

We all use this locution in conversation all the time. ("You know what they say . . . ") But in academic writing, it's always better to say just who you mean by "they".

Again, proofreading to make sure that you have said exactly what you meant to say is very, very difficult work. Reading aloud can help, as can having someone read your work— quietly to him or herself or out loud to you.

But the one tactic most likely to make a difference is taking some time away from your writing before you begin to proofread. Whether it's a couple of days, a day, or even an hour—whatever you can afford—time away will help enormously.

The Top Ten, Number Eleven?

"Nobody goes there anymore; it's too crowded."
—Yogi Berra

One of the perils of listmaking is that, inevitably, as soon as the list is finished, you think of other things that should have been on it. So, having completed our discussion of the Top Ten most common student writing problems, we need to address a few "honorable mentions".

Compound Words

Anymore and any more—

In the quotation above, Yogi uses **"anymore"** correctly, as a "time" word: in the past, folks went there, but not now.

The two words, "any more" are "amount" or "number" words:

"After his eleventh pancake, he said he couldn't possibly eat any more."

Over time and overtime—

Anybody who gets paid by the hour knows very well that **"overtime"** means "work and/or pay for work above the normal."

"Over time" is usually used to indicate gradual change:

"Over time, the 60s radicals became mainstream."

Breakup and break up—

In this pair, one is a noun, the other a verb.

"She wanted to break up with him, but somehow the breakup never quite happened."

There, Their, and They're

This is one of those writing problems in which practically everybody knows what's "right", but keeps making the mistake anyway.

And **their** doesn't seem to be any particular pattern to **they're** misuse. It's almost as if **there** determined to use the wrong one.

Then for Than

This one seems to be gaining in popularity. The way it usually works is that the writer uses "then" in a comparison:

"The CEO was more conservative **then** she should have been."

"If your team is anything other **then** supportive, you have work to do."

Both of these, of course, should be **"than"**.

Maybe this happens because we pronounce the two words more or less the same when we speak them. Just a guess . . .

P.O.V. Revisited

In *Wordworks* #27, we began a conversation about point of view in academic writing that drew some interesting responses. Also, more and more research papers are coming to the Writing Support Center, and it's pretty clear that there's more here that needs to be said.

As writers, we have our choice of which "person" to use, i.e., from which Point of View we wish to direct our message.
There are three: First, Second, and Third.

When we speak of writing in the First Person, we mean that the voice of the writing is that of the writer. The pronouns "I", "me", "my", "we", etc. appear frequently in First Person point of view.

Lots of novels, remembrances, and autobiographies are written in the First Person.

The voice in Second Person writing speaks TO the reader and uses the pronoun "You" a lot. Second Person is the least used Point of View of the three.

(It does have its uses, however. I would argue, for example, that a construction like:

"No matter what you think about her talent, you have to give her credit for trying."

is considerably more elegant than the alternative:

"No matter what one thinks about her talent, one has to give her credit for trying.")

The Third Person is (supposedly, at least) the most objective point of view. The Third Person comments on the world as distinct from both the speaker and the reader. The third person pronouns are "he", "she", "it", "they", etc.

We are told that, when writing a research paper, we should avoid the First Person, opting for the more objective Third.

And that advice can cause a common writing problem: avoiding "I" or "me" by substituting "the writer" or "the researcher".

APA style guidelines** and good writing practice agree:

DO NOT DO THIS, for the very simple reason that it can be unclear and ambiguous.

1. When reporting your opinion or recommendations, simply declare, treat your opinion as fact:

NOT: "This writer sees no promise for that technology."

INSTEAD: "That technology shows no promise."

NOT: "The researcher believes the data to be conclusive."

INSTEAD: "The data are conclusive."

2. When reporting facts, just use the first person.

NOT: "This researcher will distribute 150 surveys."

INSTEAD: "I will distribute 150 surveys."

NOT: "The researcher interviewed eight Executive Directors."

INSTEAD: "I interviewed eight Executive Directors."

(By the way, the Passive Voice-"Eight Executive Directors were interviewed."- is also a less than desirable choice.)

**American Psychological Association. (2009). *Publication Manual of the American Psychological Association* (6th ed., p. 69). Washington, DC: Author.

Picture this . . .

How do I love thee? Let me count the ways.
I love thee to the depth and breadth and height
My soul can reach, when feeling out of sight
For the ends of Being and ideal Grace.
—Elizabeth Barrett Browning, Sonnet XLIII

It's useful to remember the difference between public and private writing. Certainly, private writing (diaries, journals, love letters, etc.) is hugely important to us as human beings. But it is public writing—writing intended to be read by people who are not us and who don't necessarily know us—that we're talking about here.

Browning's famous poem is a wonderful example of abstract language. And, in a love poem written to and for a specific individual, it doesn't much matter that we can have no clue about exactly what her words mean.

But when we write for more pedestrian purposes (getting work done, reporting research results, arguing about economics, etc.) it's pretty important that our readers know exactly what we mean. So we need to avoid abstract language and look for the most concrete way we can find to make our points.

In this sentence, for example:

"When addressing management issues it is important to find sufficient driving forces behind the motivation to follow through with the plans outlined in this project."

Because the language is so abstract, we wonder, among other things:

—What **management issues**?

—Why is this important **only** when addressing management issues?

—What constitutes **"sufficient"**?

—What does **"behind the motivation"** mean?

Perhaps the writer meant something like this:

"If the team leader is to follow through with the staffing changes advocated in this report, we will need to convince him or her that the forces driving those changes are potent enough to outweigh the obstacles to the changes."

One way to make writing more concrete is to take a second look at **nouns**:

—Names and/or titles are always more concrete and clear than pronouns.

So: instead of "**They** completed the revisions in record time."

"**Sally Jones and Robert Smith** completed the revisions in record time." Or "**The audit team** completed the revisions in record time."

—Nouns that the reader can **"picture"** are always preferable. But watch out for "generic" nouns. Words like "boat", "artist", "manager", and "dog" seem at first to stand for actual things, but they really don't; they are **generic**.

You can be much surer of the "picture" in your reader's mind if you use more concrete nouns. So: Hobie Cat, Eric Clapton, Leo Durocher, and Marmaduke.

(Of course there are degrees of "concreteness." So: canoe, sculptor, CEO, and bichon frise.)

#50: What's the Good Word?"

The more you read and write, the more pleasurable it is to come across new words. These words please us for any number of reasons: they mean things we rarely have the need to express; they remind us of certain special people, places, or experiences; or they just sound nice.

The words below are the ones you submitted, plus a few of my personal favorites. See if you can match the word to its meaning. The answers are at the bottom of the page. Have fun!

1. verisimilitude   a. a stone fruit

2. logodaedalist   b. the study of the end of the world

3. catawampus   c. a mixture of unrelated styles

4. drupe   d. alignment of 3 celestial bodies

5. sesquipedalian   e. the property of resembling reality

6. eschatology   f. one skilled in word use

7. eleemosynary   g. a fierce imaginary animal

8. eclectic   h. using long words

9. conundrum   i. having to do with charity

10. syzygy   j. riddle

Answers: 1. e; 2. f; 3. g; 4. a; 5. h; 6. b; 7. i; 8. c; 9. j; 10. d.

Diner Sores

Prepositionally Speaking

Speakers and writers of the English language use thousands and thousands of words. About 150 of those words are Prepositions-but some of those (in, to, of, from, and a few others) are the words we use the most.

The word "preposition" itself describes how we use them. Prepositions are "positioned" in front of ("pre") nouns and pronouns to indicate location in time (**before** 9 o'clock, **until** later), location in space (**to** the gym, **from** the carton), or in relationship to an idea or concept (**in** a tizzy, **of** libertarian philosophy).

In some ways, these little words are difficult to discuss because their use is governed largely by custom. We don't say "a situation they currently live **within**," choosing, according to custom, "live **in**." If we wrote, "That has played an important part **of** our cohort," we'd replace the **"of"** with **"in"**.

The preposition we choose, though, does make a difference. To illustrate, here are a few examples that I've come across recently:

" . . . A must-read to guitar collectors" should be " . . . a must-read for guitar collectors".

" . . . Would result in harm of the residents" should be " . . . would result in harm to the residents".

" . . . Many effects on the elderly concerning nursing" should be " . . . many effects on the elderly from nursing".

" . . . With months of hearings, a compromise was reached" should be " . . . after months of hearings, a compromise was reached".

Many people in our part of the world (Central and Western New York State) use the phrase **"on accident"** routinely in conversation. In formal writing, of course, it should be **"by accident"**.

Finally, it used to be held that a writer could not end a sentence with a preposition, and sometimes (as a matter of clarity) it's still better not to.

But, for the most part, that proscription has gone away. Which would you choose?

"There are some things I will not put up with."

Or

"There are some things up with which I will not put."

#52: Parenthetical(s)

Over time, English has evolved a variety of shorthand ways for a writer to quietly comment, expand, elucidate, or provide examples. Using them can liven up our prose while, at the same time, making it more precise, clear, and explanatory.

In writing a sentence, it's obviously important not to wander around. But sometimes (such as right here) you will wish to insert something that is relevant "meaningwise" even if it's not entirely relevant "sentencewise".

The primary tools we have to accomplish this are dashes, parentheses, and brackets.

Dashes indicate that what is between them is in the nature of an "aside".

"Her fast—but not fast enough for her—rise to the top of the corporate ladder was the result of a lot of hard work."

"**Google**—ambitiously, one might have said—takes its name from the very large number, the *googol*: a 1 followed by 100 zeroes."

(NOTE: a **hyphen** is not the same thing as a **dash**. A hyphen is word glue: you use it to make a single modifier by sticking together several words.

Guns-on-the-table poker game; **20th-Century** man; **one-year-old** child; **not-for-profit** agency.

You also use it when you choose to spell out numbers between **twenty-one** and **ninety-nine**.)

Parentheses enclose words, phrases, sentences, or paragraphs that are technically very much off the topic, yet still comment on the topic. You can insert *parenthetical elements* into sentences, or—as in the segment above on hyphens—they can stand entirely on their own. In either case (This can require some thought.) you punctuate one as a sentence if it is one; you do not if it is not.

One word that is almost always parenthetical is "sic", a Latin word meaning "so" or "thus". We use it mostly when we are quoting another writer's words to indicate something like:

"Hey, I know he misspelled that word—or used the wrong word—and I wanted to make sure you knew I knew!" Thus:

"Pittsburgh and the nearby Ohio and Monongahela river valleys were once the center of the country's steal (sic) manufacturing."

Brackets enclose words or phrases in a quote that were not used by original writer—usually because the quote has been taken out of context. Include them in brackets to make it clear that you (not the original author) are responsible for adding them:

"It [the money] went a long way to guaranteeing the bill's passage."

" . . . supervision, goal-setting, and review [are] aspects of her job."

"Not"

" . . . negativity won't pull you through."
—Bob Dylan, "Just Like Tom Thumb's Blues"

In the rewriting process, certain words can function as signals to us that here might be a good place to think about whether we have said things as well as possible. "Not" is one of those words.

As readers, we quickly lose the thread of what we are reading if things are ill-defined or vague. So as writers it's our job to say what we mean to say, and that can be much easier said than done.

One way to try to do it is to say things positively, i.e., to define them, to declare that this or that is the case. And that's why we need to be on the lookout for the word "not".

When we write that something is NOT the case, in some instances all we have done is to eliminate one possibility out of a whole host of them, and our reader is no closer to knowing what we mean.

So, in this sentence:

"The visiting professor was **not** favorably impressed with the school's facilities."

We have a vague sense that she was—what?—disappointed? outraged? moved to sympathy? We can't tell.

Or here:

"Employees are **not** putting in an undue amount of overtime."

Is everybody going home at 5:00? Are they working overtime, but not a lot? Is business way off? Are they choosing not to work extra? Who knows?

One more:

"He will **not** look for a job."

So what WILL he do? Go on welfare? Keep the job he has? Turn to a life of crime?

(NOTE: "Not" can be used for emphasis, if we follow with a positive statement, thus:

"He will **not** look for a job; rather he **will** try his luck and talent as a freelancer in the global, internet marketplace.")

Language is a Treacherous Thing

" . . .language is a treacherous thing, a most unsure vehicle."
—Mark Twain

Some of the people I admire most are those who can speak and write in several languages. And I am especially in awe of those who have learned English as a "foreign" language; it can be so confusing!

"Affect" and "Effect" are prime examples of just how confusing. Most of the time, of course, the meanings of the two words are pretty straightforward.

"Affect" (with the accent on the second syllable) is a **verb**. It means something like "influence" or "alter", as in:

"Extremes of climate **affect** different crops in different ways."

"Effect" (also accented on the second syllable) is a **noun**. It means "result" or "what was caused".

"She insisted that the wine had no **effect** on her whatsoever."

"The real problem was that they didn't think through the possible **effects** of their decision."

But, sometimes . . .

"Effect" can be a **verb**. As a verb, it is almost always used in the sense of causing some change or other.

"In order to **effect** a more orderly transition, the president promoted certain individuals and transferred others."

"They were desperate to **effect** a change in their living situation."

Likewise . . .

"Affect" (accent on the first syllable) is a **noun** with several related meanings, all having to do with "appearance".

"Certain diseases can result in a person losing **affect**; i.e., her face stays the same regardless of what emotion she is feeling."

"Affect" can also mean **"affectation"**-putting on the appearance of something one is not.

"His ten-gallon hat, boots, and spurs gave him a "cowboy" **affect**, even though he was born and bred in Greenwich Village."

Sailing, sailing . . .

A hallmark of our English language is that it is always changing. Moreover, those changes tend to happen in the language of everyday people first, then work their way "up" until they become used in formal communications. Words come into the language from everywhere and often change meanings as they are absorbed. Finding out where words we use all the time came from (a.k.a. their "etymology") can be fun.

For thousands of years, before trains (early 1800s), planes (early 1900s), and automobiles (late 1800s), sailing ships provided the fastest way to transport people and goods over long distances.
Sailing ships were designed as cargo vessels, passenger carriers, and pleasure craft. They were also the most powerful weapons of war.

Charles Darwin based his *On the Origin of Species* on what he had discovered on his voyage aboard the HMS Beagle. A guy called Edward Teach became the pirate Blackbeard, an early celebrity outlaw, thanks to sailing ships. And who knows how different things would be today had Senor Columbus not sailed west from Spain on his Nina, Pinta, and Santa Maria?

England became the most powerful and wealthiest nation on earth primarily because she ruled the waves. And not only her coffers were enriched, but her language was too. Indeed, a whole host of terms that we use in everyday speech and writing have--often forgotten--nautical origins.

Bitter end: This term originally referred to the end of a ship's anchor cable that is attached to the ship. "Bitter" here is not the opposite of "sweet"; rather it signifies that the cable was secured to the ship at a pair of posts called "bitts".

By and large: We use this expression to mean something like "from any way you look at a thing." And its nautical meaning is related. When a ship is "by", it is sailing as closely as possible to the direction from which the wind is blowing. When "large", it is sailing with the breeze directly astern.

Three Sheets to the Wind: Despite their physical resemblance to bed-sheets, sails are not called "sheets". A sheet, rather, is the sailing term for a rope that controls a sail. Thus, if three sheets are blowing in the wind, the ship is out of control. No wonder the phrase came to mean "extremely intoxicated".

Leeway: A sailing ship, unlike a railroad train, does not run on tracks. And as it is moved by the wind, it must necessarily be blown at least a little bit sideways even as it moves forward on its course. The wind blows at the ship from the "weather" side; the other side is the "lee" side. "Leeway", then, is the distance between the ship and the nearest land on the lee side--enough room to try something different or even make a mistake and not worry about crashing into a rock.

Know the Ropes: Everything from keeping the masts standing upright to stretching certain sails in the right direction, to providing ladders was accomplished on a sailing ship by hundreds of ropes. A young crewman had to learn what they all did--he had to "learn the ropes"-- while an experienced sailor was said to "know the ropes".

Footloose: With all due respect to Kenny Wormald and Kevin Bacon, the origin of this term has nothing to do with dancing or even human feet. The bottom portion of a sail is called the "foot". If the foot is unsecured (by ropes, naturally!), the sail flaps in the wind and cannot be made to do its duty.

(NOTE: If you enjoy this sort of thing, you might like a book called *A Sea of Words,* by Dean King, et.al., Henry Holt & Co., 1995.)

Only Part of the Story

I once heard (probably in an undergraduate art history class, but I'm not sure anymore) that Pablo Picasso had mastered the techniques of classical figure drawing by the time he was 12. So that when he broke the rules, so to speak, it was intentional and done out of mastery. The same goes for pretty much all of the elements of good writing: a master knows when and why to ignore the conventions to achieve a specific effect—but the rest of us might better play it safe.

Q: What do these three sentences have in common?

"Recent incidents of faulty evidence analysis whether they are eyewitness evidence or lab evidence; one or both will either cancel each other out dismissing a case and letting the free go or they will help each other out to serve as useful pieces of evidence to also free the innocent or imprison the guilty."

"Interventions such as learning as much as possible about the illnesses, prognoses, and available treatments, knowing the clients' family support systems and their views, realizing that the clients who are near death often need helping coping with their psychological pain and physical suffering, assuming the role of a resource person, helping clients understand the importance of various personal and formal documents, and most importantly offering comfort to loved ones and friends after the death."

"A growing number of retailers as the growth in the field of e-commerce, which is shifting toward sites that sell goods directly to consumers over those that focus on bartering between individuals."

A: While they all begin with upper-case letters and end with periods, none of them is a sentence; they are all **sentence fragments.**

A sentence is an idea or the description of an event. It is a bit like a VERY short story in which some person or thing (the subject) does something (the verb) to some other person or thing (the object). ("He smokes a cigarette.")

And while a sentence (story) can indeed get along without an object ("He smokes."), it cannot be complete without a subject ("Smokes a cigarette.") or a verb ("He a cigarette.").

And that is true, as the examples above illustrate, no matter how many words the writer uses.

As for those examples:

#1 is complicated because the bit following the semicolon is indeed a complete sentence, while the part before it is just a noun with descriptors.

#2 gives a bunch of examples of "interventions" with no verb to complete the thought.

#3 feels to me more like a proofreading error than anything else. It seems that a verb belongs after the word "retailers".

Sometimes, to be sure, you may (in honor of Picasso?) wish to use fragments intentionally. For emphasis. But only sometimes. And very carefully. Without getting carried away.

Screamers, et. al.

The fact that punctuation is profoundly important in writing is nearly self-evident. The inclusion or placement of even the lowly comma can make all the difference.

These sentences from Lynne Truss's *Eats, Shoots, and Leaves** have very different meanings, even though the words don't change, only the commas:

"The people in line who managed to get tickets were very happy."

"The people in line, who managed to get tickets, were very happy."

In the first sentence only some folks got tickets, but everybody in the second sentence is going to the game.

Then there's this famous example:

"Charles the First walked and talked half an hour after his head was cut off."

. . . which is far more disquieting than the punctuated version: "Charles the First walked and talked; half an hour after, his head was cut off."

So we really could not write very clearly without the common punctuation: commas, periods, semi-colons, colons, and question marks.

But what about those other punctuation marks? Let's consider how we're supposed to use square brackets ([ ]), curly brackets ({ }), ellipses (. . .), and, above all, exclamation points (!).

Square Brackets usually signify that we have changed something in a quote to make it clear or to make it fit in a sentence. So:

"The reporter tried all day to interview [former] President Carter."

"I could not see how 'add[ing] another row of seats' would solve the problem."

You won't use Curly Brackets (sometimes called "braces") very much at all, but there they are on your keyboard, right? I'm told that they're useful in math, but in writing they pretty much only enclose a series of equal choices, thus:

"Grab your garment {coat, sweater, jacket, cape} and we'll head out."

An **Ellipsis** (aka "dot, dot, dot") indicates that something is missing. So when you are writing a research paper and you want to include a quote but the whole thing is too long, use an ellipsis to show that you've taken stuff out:

"The use of computers and robotics promises to . . . enhance the ability to learn new complex operations."

(NOTE: there's a space between each dot in an ellipsis— space dot space dot space dot space.)

Exclamation Points (in the ad agency business, at least) are often called "Screamers". And the best advice is to use them sparingly. They indicate that what comes before is an exclamation, and exclamations are pretty rare, especially in academic prose.

"I can't believe you just said that!" or "Wow!"

Most importantly, resist the temptation to add some zip to an otherwise humdrum sentence by ending it with a screamer. It will be obvious to your reader that that's what you're up to.

*Truss, L. (2004). *Eats, shoots, and leaves*. Profile Books.

Words That Ain't Words . . . Yet

"Ain't" ain't a word. Right? But, of course, it is one; we use it all the time. It's conversational English. And though we wouldn't use it in formal academic writing now, the way our language constantly changes, someday we probably will.

The word "Diction" refers to the words we choose to use when we speak or write. Academic writing requires formal diction. And even that is a moving target; lots of the words we might use in formal writing today would have been considered too informal a generation ago. (Contractions are a convenient example.)

Some "nonwords" have been all but eliminated by word processors and spell check. Time was, for example, that many, many essays contained the "words" "alot", "definately", "perservere", and "sherbert"--but not so much anymore.

But there are several that are actually increasing in frequency; probably, over the long term, some are destined to become acceptable in formal prose. For now, however, it would be best to avoid them.

Alright is not, technically, a word. The idea it expresses is correctly written as two words, thus: all right.

Orientated/Disorientated both add the unnecessary syllable. At "orientation" you got "oriented", not "orientated". (Just as when you made your presentation, you "presented"; you didn't "presentate".)

Ginormous is a delightful coinage that does a great job in conversation. It's probably on its way to the formal category, but it's not (it ain't?) there yet.

Irregardless means the same thing as regardless. So why the extra "ir"? Nobody knows, but for some who hear it or read it (you know who you are!), it's nails on a chalkboard. (Remember chalkboards?)

Okay phonetically translates the (correct) O.K. or OK and makes it into something that kind of looks like a word. But it's not one.

Flustrated is another very useful coinage, and, like ginormous, could be on its way to respectability. How better to quickly express a condition that is a combination of flustered and frustrated?

Was like, followed by a quote, is one of those wonderful (conversational) speech patterns that, while defying grammatical logic, manage to convey a great deal.

"When I walked in late to the party, he was like, 'Oh, you decided to show up.'"

This efficiently communicates so much more than the (more correct) alternative, "he said." It captures not only his words, but also his attitude, his nature, and to some extent the whole gestalt.
But don't write it in an essay.

#59: Homonyms

There really is something about our English language that is positively perverse.

These sentences, for example, are all correct:

I would like to **lie** down for a nap.

She told me to **lay** the package on the floor.

Last night, she finally **lay** down to sleep after midnight.

I **laid** the book on the desk.

He has **lain** on the couch for three days.

She has **laid** the crucial groundwork.

Further complicating things is the fact that, like most languages, English started out as a spoken language, long before we figured out how to write it down. And we still use "speech" words when talking about writing:

What did the article **say**? How does that sentence **sound** to you?

So when words that mean very different things sound alike, that can cause problems. Those words are called "homonyms".

Peak, **Peek**, and **Pique**

 "**Peak**" describes rising diagonals that meet to form a point, as in high mountains or the roofs of houses.

To "**Peek**" is to look quickly and surreptitiously. (Are there any better games than "Peek-A-Boo"?)

"**Pique**" has several meanings, but they are all related to "excite":

My constant badgering finally aroused her pique (anger).

A peek at the peak piqued my interest in the architecture.

Allusion and **Illusion**

These words aren't pronounced exactly the same, but close enough to confuse.

An "**allusion**" is a reference to something else:

"His argument contained an allusion to Emma Lazarus's Statue of Liberty poem."

An "**illusion**" is an idea that is wrong:

"Three weeks in Iraq dispelled most of her illusions about the nobility of warfare."

Elicit and **Illicit**

"**Elicit**" means to draw out:

"The lawyer's objective in her cross examination was to elicit the truth."

"**Illicit**" means not legal or against the rules:

"He lost his job because of his illicit use of company equipment."

Capital and **Capitol**

"**Capital**" means money (as in "Das Kapital"); it is the root word of "Capitalism".

It also means the *city* that is the seat of government.

The central official government *building* is often called the **Capitol**.

The capital of Pennsylvania is Harrisburg, where you can see the beautiful Capitol dome.

Able was I ere I saw Elba

One thing that will help us all to be better writers is to pay attention to words as words. Several previous *Wordworks* have focused on what words mean, but this week we're going to look at, of all things, the sequence of letters in words and sentences. It's more fun that you might think!

A "hippodrome" is a racecourse. ("Hippos" is the Greek word for "horse": e.g., "hippopotamus" = "river horse".)

But that does not mean that a "Palindrome" is a racetrack for former vice-presidential candidates. On the contrary, a palindrome is any sequence of characters that reads the same backwards and forwards.

Certain names are palindromes: Bob, Otto, Lil.

Numbers can be palindromes, too: 101; 23,432; 77; 8,923,298.

(Obviously, each century contains only one palindromic year. Most of us alive now have had the fairly unusual experience of living through two: 1991 and 2002.)

The most entertaining palindromes, though, are those that (even sort of) mean something . . . like the vaguely Napoleonic lament that is the subject line of this post.

Another pretty famous one supposedly refers to Teddy Roosevelt:

"A man, a plan, a canal: Panama."

Then there's the theologian's puzzle:

"Do geese see God?"

Or the exasperated trattoria customer to his waiter:

"Go hang a salami; I'm a lasagna hog."

Here's the longest one I know of. It's not the most cogent, but it is long:

"Doc note: I dissent. A fast never prevents a fatness. I diet on cod."

Finally, my personal favorite, the anti-commercialism dictum:

"Trade ye no mere moneyed art."

Inherently Vague

Pronouns, those words that stand in for nouns, are indispensable. Just imagine how difficult it would be to write or to read if we had to repeat nouns over and over.

"Joe wanted to clean out Joe's car so Joe pulled Joe's car in to the garage and opened the doors of Joe's car. Then Joe emptied Joe's car out and dumped the garbage into the garbage can so that the garbage wouldn't be all over the floor."

You get the idea.

Useful as they are, though, because they are inherently vague, pronouns need to be used with care.

Organizations

Even though they are composed (not "comprised") of many people, we refer to organizations by singular pronouns, not plural: an organization is an "it" not a "they".

"Keuka College welcomed more than 200 students to its ASAP program."

"Ford still makes the world's most popular truck. It sells its F-150 model in every country."

(It needs to be said here that this is true of American English. In British English, it's just the opposite:

"Keuka College welcomed more than 200 students to their ASAP program."

Go figure.)

Who or **That**?

The answer to this dilemma is often a judgment call. But, in general, it just makes sense to use "who" when you are talking about people (especially specific people), and "that" when not.

"Parents who opt to home school their children have a long list of challenges to overcome."

"Samuel Johnson, who compiled the first English dictionary, was famous for his punning ability."

"The committee decided to discuss only those matters that could be dealt with on the spot."

But what about animals? My dog is a "who", not a "that", right?

The simple answer is the best: if the animal has a name, it's "who"; if not, it's "that".

"The bison that had been so diminished by wanton hunting are slowly gaining in numbers."

"She brought her cat, who yowled continuously, into the vet's examination room."

Grammar Jargon

It can be delightful to find out what things are really called. And in practical terms, it's handy when talking about a technical subject to be able to call things by their right names.

Grammar is surely a technical subject, and its jargon is no less useful (or potentially confusing) than that of any other technical subject. So check these out, just for the fun of it. They may or may not bring back fond high school memories. There will be no quiz.

Parts of Speech

Words belong to different classifications, depending on their function in a sentence. Each class of word has a name, and collectively we call those classes the **Parts of Speech**. They are:

Noun (person, place or thing), Pronoun (substitute for a noun), Verb (action word), Adjective (describes a noun or pronoun), Adverb (describes a verb or adjective), Preposition (direction word), Conjunction (and, but, or, nor, etc.), and Interjection (Yo!).

Verbals

Verbs turn into other parts of speech in various ways; these verbs that are not verbs are called "Verbals."

An **Infinitive** is a noun based on a verb; it adds a "to" in front of the verb, thus: to sing, to dance, to consider.

(Some people frown on what are known as "split infinitives" in which something comes between the "to" and the verb: "to soberly consider" should be "to consider soberly".)

Another verbal that is really a noun is called a **Gerund**; add "ing" to the verb, as in: **Cooking** is easy. **Writing** is hard. **Studying** gets in the way.

Verbals can be adjectives, too. **Participles** look just like **Gerunds** (adding the "ing"), but they modify: **scorching** heat, **calming** words, **peeling** paint.

(NOTE: "Dangling Participles" ought, I think, to be called "Dangling Gerunds." But whatever you call them, it is well to be on the lookout for them and fix them when you find them.

Here's one: "By **analyzing** the progress, it will help decide about staffing." Should be: "**Analyzing** the process will help decide about staffing."

The Moods

Your boss isn't the only one who's moody; your sentences are, too.

There's the **Declarative Mood** that states a fact. ("You **are** here.") There's the **Imperative Mood** that tells us what to do. ("**Get out** of here.") There's the **Interrogative Mood** that asks a question. ("**Why are** you here?") And there's the **Subjunctive Mood** that wonders "what if?" ("If I **were** here, **would** you be too?)

Right Out There in Public

"Sign, sign, everywhere a sign
Blockin' out the scenery, breakin' my mind
Do this, don't do that, can't you read the sign?"
—Les Emmerson, Five Man Electrical Band

It's pretty eye-opening to take note of the number and frequency of writing mistakes in public and commercial communications: menus, brochures, packaging, posters, and signs.

One category of communications mistakes should surely be classified as typos. And most of these are simple spelling errors.

Like the sign on the vacant restaurant in the village where I live:

"BDLG for Lease or Sale"

Not really sure what a "BDLG" is.

A local pizza joint printed thousands of paper take-home menus touting its "Traditional Italian Cusine." (The sign in the window has it right, thankfully: cuisine.)

This will not surprise anyone who's ever worked in advertising or publications. There is no doubt that the most likely place for a typo is in a headline or title: we tend to scrutinize tiny footnote type, assuming that the headline must be right. And, as we all know about proofreading our own work, we see what we think should be there rather than what is actually there.

. . . as in this page header from a college financial aid brochure:

"The Free Application for Federal Sudent Aid (FAFSA)."

Punctuation problems constitute the next category of mistakes you see out in the world; lots of them involve apostrophes.

"Now Hiring: Service Tech's"

These kinds of mistakes are particularly noticeable when they're made by someone who knows better. So the folks who belong to the Poetry Club at a certain area Community College ought to be embarrassed by their poster:

"The Poetry Club is calling for members and poetry submissions for it's student magazine."

All of the public schools in my city display banners that proclaim, **"We Can Make A Difference"**. Why did they put the sentence in quotes? Who said it?

The Final category of signage mistakes comes under the heading of using the wrong word.

For example, we're all familiar with the supermarket express lane that limits patrons to "7 Items or Less". The sign should, of course, read, "7 Items or Fewer".

Just last week, I noticed a printed window banner at a discount clothing retailer that read, **"Find New Fashions EVERYDAY"**.

What the store really means to say is "Find New Fashions Every Day".

I recently purchased a 45-roll package of toilet paper at a local warehouse store. (The package always says "bathroom tissue", but I never heard anybody call it anything but "toilet paper", did you?)

Printed on the package are the words:

"Our Largest Everyday Package!".

And I wonder what that means. Presumably, they sell an even larger package of special occasion tissue. Hard to imagine, though.

And, by the way, why add the exclamation point?

Paragraphs

Over the years, I've heard from many students that their high school English teachers told them that each paragraph must have 4 sentences. (Some say 3; some say 5.) Those students are usually dismayed when I inform them that this is simply not true.

There's no such thing as a paragraph that is too long or too short. The most important thing about paragraphs is NOT how many sentences each contains; no, the important thing to stay aware of is that each paragraph has only ONE TOPIC.

When you start a new topic, start a new paragraph.

Each paragraph is like a small essay and as such has a beginning, a middle, and an end. It begins (like an essay) by letting the reader know what it's about.

So the first or second sentence of your paragraph is its TOPIC sentence. Here's an example:

"I feel that our cohort group functions quite well already, even though we have only known each other for about three months."

As readers, we know what the paragraph will be about. The main idea of the paragraph is how the cohort functions well as a group.

The "middle" section of the paragraph should provide explanation via definitions, details, clarification, or examples, to add dimension to what the writer is communicating.

So, she continues:

"We get along with each other, are comfortable with each other, work well together and function effectively as a group. To my knowledge, there are no personal or group conflicts within our group."

The "end" of the paragraph lets us know that the discussion of this topic is finished. In this example, though, the writer uses the final sentence to present another angle on her topic, one that does help conclude the discussion:

"Our experiment with game theory during our last class was very divisive, but I hope that was a temporary condition and part of our overall learning experience."

And here's the whole paragraph:

"I feel that our cohort group functions quite well already, even though we have only known each other for about three months. We get along with each other, are comfortable with each other, work well together and function effectively as a group. To my knowledge, there are no personal or group conflicts within our group. Our experiment with game theory during our last class was very divisive, but I hope that was a temporary condition and part of our overall learning experience."

The writer next talks about what she anticipates will develop as her cohort moves through the program. But that's a new topic, and so she does it in a new paragraph.

Tips of the Slung

Listening to an NPR story on the 2012 Florida Republican Primary, I heard the reporter identify one of the candidates as "Ritt Momney". He immediately corrected himself, but I got to thinking about these kinds of slips of the tongue, and remembered about Spoonerisms—and other amusing varieties of wordplay.

English contains somewhere around 620,000 words, many more than any other language. That makes a whole range of humorous word use (and mistakes) so much easier and so much more likely.

Spoonerisms

"Spoonerisms" take their name from the Rev. W.A. Spooner (1844-1930), Dean and Warden of New College at Oxford, England. Spooner was famous for swapping word sounds to make humorous and, sometimes, telling new phrases: like the time he told a student who had spent the semester having a good time at the expense of his studies that he had "Tasted the Worm!"

Examples of Spoonerisms are pretty much endless. Some of the better ones:

In a toast to Queen Victoria, Spooner is reputed to have said, "Three cheers for our queer old dean."

During WWI, he announced, "When our boys come home from France, we shall have the hags flung out."

And he referred to England's farmers as "Noble tons of soil."

Oxymorons

"Oxymorons", of course, are phrases that contradict themselves. They are usually amusing and sometimes make a strange kind of sense—even poetry.

John Milton in *Paradise Lost*, for example, described Hell as "darkness visible".

Then there are the more or less famous oxymorons: military intelligence, jumbo shrimp, paid volunteer, and Microsoft works.

Malapropisms

In his 1775 comedy, *The Rivals*, playwright Richard Brinsley Sheridan introduced the world to Mrs. Malaprop. She got laughs from such lines as, " . . . illiterate (should be obliterate) him from your memory," and "she's as headstrong as an allegory (instead of alligator) on the banks of the Nile."

So a malapropism is simply use of a wrong--but similar sounding--word. These can be pretty funny:

Like the worker who describes his colleague as a vast suppository of knowledge.

Or the officer who complained of the personnel "spreading dysentery among the ranks."

Words to Watch For - VII

"I shoulda' learned to play the guitar;
I shoulda' learned to play them drums."
—Dire Straits, "Money for Nothing"

As we have noted before many times, English Word Usage can be devilishly tricky. Informal word usage becomes accepted formal diction; words fall by the wayside; and we find that some words that we use all the time don't mean what we thought they meant.

Strait/Straight

The word "strait" isn't used too much anymore. It means something like "a very tight (even uncomfortably tight) situation."

It is also a geography word—"Straits of Magellan", "Straits of Hormuz"— denoting narrow sea lanes.

Otherwise, it shows up mostly in compounds like "straitjacket" and "straitlaced" or to describe a desperate, even deadly, state of affairs (or, indeed, a great rock band) as "dire straits".

It is important not to confuse the word with its homonym, "Straight".

Being that/Being as

These phrases are, to some degree, regionalisms: in some parts of the country folks say things like, "Being that the teacher was late, most of the students left before class started."

This is conversational English, best to avoid in formal writing. It is much better, when you need to show a cause and effect relationship, to use cause and effect words like "since", "because" and "so".

"Because the teacher was late, most of the students left before class started."

Or

"The teacher was late, so most of the students left before class started."

Mettle/Metal/Medal/Meddle

"Mettle" means a certain kind of resilient courage, and is almost always used in sentences like, "The soldier's mettle was tested by the long battle."

The trick is never to confuse it with any of those words with which it rhymes (or almost rhymes).

Nauseated/Nauseous

I have a hard time remembering to use the right word in this pair. When you feel like throwing up, you are nauseated, not nauseous.

"Nauseous", in fact, means something close to "nauseating"—making you feel like throwing up.

So, that lunch that you left in the car trunk four months ago is nauseous; you, as a result, are nauseated.

(Just for the record, I am being overly pedantic here. Lots of highly articulate people use "nauseous" to mean the same thing as "nauseated". They are wrong.)

Downfall

I see this word misused a lot. It does not mean "mistake" or "error".

It does mean "utter ruin":

"The Iowa caucuses accurately predicted the candidate's downfall."

It can also mean something like "fatal flaw":

"A habit of procrastination was his downfall."

Adviser/Advisor

Good news! You can't go wrong here.

These are simply alternative spellings of the same word. Take your pick; both are correct!

#67: Spring Training Special

Major League Baseball's Spring Training begins each February. And what those ballplayers (more than 433 of whom are each paid more than $1,000,000 to play) will be spending their time doing is brushing up on the basics: fielding ground balls, hitting the cutoff man, laying down bunts. Spring Training is perhaps the ultimate recognition of the incredible importance of thinking about and practicing fundamentals.

To be a successful college student, you must also be a successful college writer. Of course that means getting the grammar and punctuation right, correctly following APA (or MLA or U of Chicago) Style, using appropriate research sources and citing them, and making sure you accurately and adequately complete the assignment. You can find out about all of that elsewhere, and you certainly should. What I want to review here are some very basic guidelines.

Title Everything

A good title encapsulates or comments on what's in your paper. And, as we know, you only get one chance to make a good first impression.

Make a Good Beginning

Your reader will be much more likely to follow what you're up to if you make it clear right from the beginning what you're writing about and why, in what context you are writing, and what your method will be.

Academic Writing Differs from Writing for Work

In the writing we do for work, we use bulleted points; we keep things brief and to the point; and the content may reflect a company's or industry's point of view.

In Academic Writing, the format is structured; in-depth analysis is required; ideas must be explained and supported; content is research based.

Four Steps to Writing with "Style"

1. Assume that your reader knows nothing about your topic.
2. Write the way you talk.
3. Clean it up (for grammar, spelling, etc.).
4. Don't try for sophistication; try for "real." (Eschew obfuscation.)

Writing is Rewriting

Getting words onto a page is useful inasmuch as it gives you something to work on. It's the work that you do on those words that results in quality writing. Each formal paper or essay that you submit for a course should go through several drafts before you hand it over to your instructor.

Subheads Are Magic

Identify the sections of your paper by using subheads. They'll let your reader know what's going on in the most economical way.

Proofread, Proofread, Proofread

Sending a letter or an email that you obviously didn't bother to proofread conveys two messages to your reader: 1. this information wasn't all that important; and 2. you aren't all that important. And the same is true of any work that you turn in for one of your courses. Bottom line: those are not the messages you want to send to your instructors.

Email Best Practices

For many of us, e-mail has become the default communications method, for work and school at any rate. Clearly, that's because it works so well: it allows us to take care of things efficiently; it leaves a record; it gives us the chance to craft our messages so they have maximum effect and clarity.

Email can also be annoying. And, if not used carefully, it can have disastrous effects. The following list is the result of many, many conversations with students, colleagues, and clients. The list of Email Best Practices is always open for comment, editing, and input. But it's a place to start. Let me know if you have any "Best Practices" that should be added.

When you communicate via e-mail . . .

- Be concise and to the point.
- Answer all questions your reader may have and pre-empt further questions.
- Use proper spelling, grammar, and punctuation, and do not trust Spell Check or Grammar Check.
- Make it personal.
- Always use a meaningful subject line, putting topic first.
- Answer swiftly.
- Do not write in all CAPITALS or use various and/or colored fonts.
- Don't leave out the message thread. Also: don't start new; continue with old thread. Conversely, don't start a new conversation with an old thread.
- Read the email before you send it. (Hint: Fill in the "To" line last.)
- Do not overuse "Reply to All."
- Do not use email to discuss confidential information or to address conflicts.

Finally, don't use email when another communications tool (the phone, a formal letter, a face-to-face meeting) will do a better job.

#69: Plagiarism F.A.Q.s

A few years ago, to help prepare myself to give a brief presentation on plagiarism, I did what I—and, I expect, most people—always do: I Googled. My search term was the single word "plagiarism," and I was amazed at the results, which--on the first page, at least--consisted of site after site offering term papers for sale . . . cheap!

I relate this story to underscore the central reality of plagiarism in the internet age: it is so easy to do. (Those of a certain age will recall a time when, in order to plagiarize, you had to do a lot of typing.) And it takes many forms, all the way from the obvious cheating involved in patronizing one of those term paper mills to the much less serious failure to properly cite a source.

So:

Q1: What is Plagiarism?

Webster's online dictionary defines "plagiarism" as: "A piece of writing that has been copied from someone else and is presented as being your own work." That's pretty clear, right? So plagiarism involves stealing (copying) and lying (presented as your own work).
That's why plagiarism is treated so seriously by the college.

Q2: What information do I need to cite

To some extent, this is a judgment call—because it involves deciding whether what I have written is "common knowledge" or not. This can be tricky, but it's usually fairly easy to determine. Everybody knows that Abraham Lincoln gave a speech called "The Gettysburg Address"—that's common knowledge. Not everybody likely knows that on the day of the speech, those in attendance, Lincoln included, thought that the speech had been a flop.

Q3: My teacher said I cited too much. How could that be?

When the paper you submit consists of one quote after another, with very little of your own thinking, you can't really say that you have "written" anything. While your citations and References page may be laudably accurate and complete, what you have done is assemble other people's writing. In writing for college, it's important that most of what you write represent your own thinking, opinions, experience, and analysis; you'll want to use other people's writing only to support your own position or to substantiate facts.

#70: It's Only Words . . .

"It's only words,
And words are all I have
To take your heart away."
—The BeeGees

You can't know too many words, right? Sure, you can always consult a Thesaurus to find another word to replace one that you don't want to overuse, but that can be dangerous: words that mean nearly the same thing may carry different suggestive meanings (called "connotations") that can trip you up. So it's better just to use words you know--and, again, the more the better!

Here are some little-used words that you may know. Match the word with the definition that most nearly fits. Find the answers at the bottom of the page. Good luck and have fun!

1. Aught
   - a. Should
   - b. Anything
   - c. Eight
   - d. Bad
2. Scabrous
   - a. Obscene
   - b. Ripe
   - c. Full of scabs
   - d. Ancient
3. Victual
   - a. Not actual
   - b. Like a victim
   - c. Accusatory
   - d. Food

4.   Uxorious
  a. Greedy
  b. Overweight
  c. Foolishly affectionate
  d. Rhythmic

5. Aplomb
  a. Self-possession
  b. All together
  c. Uncooked
  d. Despair

6.   Gerrymander
  a. Wander aimlessly
  b. Prepare dessert
  c. Sing out of tune
  d. Redistrict

Answers: 1-b, 2-a, 3-d, 4-c, 5-a, 6-d

Successful Presentations I

"What'd I say?"
—Ray Charles

I read in *Business Week* magazine several years ago that something like 33,000,000 presentations get made in the U.S. every day. Why do I suspect that most of them are terrible?

No matter what the profession, it's fair to say that a **great** presenter with a **mediocre** idea is far more likely to succeed than a **mediocre** presenter with a **great** idea. So it's probably worth a few minutes to think about some things that can get in the way of great presentations.

Fear

Every so often, the "what do you fear most" surveys (there are lots) are conducted, and over the years "public speaking" always comes in first or second. ("Death" typically comes in somewhere around sixth.)

But **knowledge conquers fear.** I.e., if you really feel like you know way more about your topic than your audience does, you'll be lots less afraid. Hard work getting to know your facts and practice, practice, practice will make you a star.

(By the way, that's not to say you shouldn't be nervous, because you probably should be. Everybody is nervous, even if they don't necessarily look it. A little touch of nerves means you care and makes you sharp.)

Bad Visuals

Well at the top of this category sits the fabled "death by PowerPoint" committed by presenters who read their slides to their audiences. Not only is this practice unutterably boring, but it is also profoundly insulting—as though your audience is so limited that they must be read to, even though the words are right there on the screen.

One of the best PowerPoints I ever saw contained no words at all, just a series of well-chosen photographs that powerfully symbolized the speaker's points and to which she was able to speak.

The best visuals, I would argue, are actual, **three-dimensional objects.** I could talk all day, with pictures, about how a bike helmet could save your life, but you will remember my point much better if I hold up a cracked bike helmet and tell you about the head inside that was spared.

(NOTE: resist the temptation to pass things around the room or to give your audience notes or a printed PowerPoint outline during your presentation. **You** need to be everyone's focal point, and anything that competes with you for attention is bad. Give them stuff at the end.)

Unclear Focus

Your audience needs to know, right up front, exactly what this presentation is about. So, just as in an essay, **articulate your thesis** right away: What is my subject? What is my attitude toward my subject? What will be my method?

And, as much as you can, think hard about what your audience knows and cares about—where are they "coming from"? About the worst thing that can happen would be for some guy in the back row to wonder to himself, halfway through, "when is she going to start talking about **me**?"

Writing for College

#72: What's Another Word for . . .

One of the really wonderful things about our English language is the multiplicity of words—especially slang words—for the same thing or idea. Regional, cultural, class, nationality, generational, and other differences contribute to the rich mix.

A "synonym" is a word that can be substituted for another word. And it's fun to take a look at certain words, just to see how many ways there are to say the same thing. Lots of synonyms grow out of everyday use; some are jargon; a few are little one- or two-word poems.

Here are a few words that have attracted lots of synonyms. I'll bet you know more for each of them that I didn't think of!

Coffee

Battery acid, bean juice, java, Americano, brew, caffeine, cuppa, leaded/unleaded, mud, mocha, and joe.

Toilet

Bathroom, convenience, head, privy, crapper, bog, john, gents/ladies, water closet/w.c., loo, throne, lavatory, can, jakes, closet, latrine, pissoir, washroom, and outhouse.

152

Car

Auto, rod, bucket, buggy, clunker, conveyance, heap, jalopy, junker, limousine, machine, motor, motorcar, pickup, ride, roadster, wheels, and wreck.

Money

Loot, cash, bucks, swag, dinero, dead presidents, lucre, dough, clams, bread, moolah, pelf, simoleons, beans, skins, and fun tickets.

Jail

Calaboose, slammer, big house, inside, lockup, brig, nick, stir, cooler, hoosegow, joint, jug, pokey, pen, and (my favorite) crowbar hotel.

Keep It Together

"Convoluted", "complicated", and "dense" are often fitting adjectives for what passes as sophisticated writing. But they are rarely fitting descriptions of good writing. Indeed, good writers work very hard to make their writing clear, straightforward, and easy to follow.

The most basic English sentence consists of a subject, a verb, and an object: some person or thing does something to some other person or thing. And the truth is that sentences that keep those parts together, as a unit, tend to be clearer than sentences that let those parts wander around and get mixed up with modifiers, limiters, categorizers, and other sentence elements that, despite the best intentions, can really lose your reader.

So, for example:

My cat **killed** a **mouse.**

This sentence really could not be clearer. That's not to say it couldn't be more interesting. But, in adding interest, it's a good idea not to disturb that three-part unit. So:

My fifteen-year-old calico **cat killed** a **mouse** on the back steps and brought it into the house during dinner.

That's a lot clearer than something like:

My **cat**, who is fifteen years old and calico, brought in to the house during dinner a **mouse** she had **killed** on the back steps.

And that's because that three-part unit has been lost.

Another example:

Barack **Obama made** a **speech**.

Again, not that interesting, but clear as crystal.

Reacting to criticism from a variety of sources both in and outside of his own party, President Barack **Obama made** a **speech** in which he defended his actions with respect to Afghanistan.

Because that **subject-verb-object** unit remains intact, the sentence is still clear, but lots more interesting and informative. Disaster strikes when each of those three parts goes off on its own:

President Barack **Obama**, reacting to criticism from a variety of sources both in and outside of his own party **made** the defense of his actions with respect to Afghanistan the topic of a **speech**.

The takeaway here, I think, is: when you're proofreading your work, and you come across a sentence that just isn't working, that seems convoluted and confusing, find that **subject, verb, and object.** Then put them together as a unit and let everything else relate to that unit.

It really works.

#74:

Change is the only constant.

"Time may change me."
—David Bowie

When I was younger, the phrase "hook up" meant something like, "join" or "become acquainted with". But a few weeks ago, after I suggested to a crowd of visiting families that anybody who wanted to could "hook up" with a tour guide outside the auditorium, I was made aware that the meaning of that phrase has changed. Won't make that mistake again!

The English language is constantly changing, and that is one of its chief glories. Words change meanings; they can become different parts of speech; what was grammatically unthinkable becomes correct and usual. Best of all, those changes tend to be bottom up rather than top down. The language of everyday conversation and discourse--of "the street"--becomes, over time, acceptable in formal speech and writing.

Gone, but not quite forgotten

Of course, there are many, many words that were once common that we don't use at all anymore. You run into them in Charles Dickens and Jane Austen novels.

It used to be, for example, that if you wanted to go shopping, you might have said, "I would **fain** go shopping."

Or if the student would not hear of any opposition to her plan, she might have expressed it as, "I will not be **gainsaid**."

We no longer say **hark** when we mean **listen**. We no longer say **twain** when we mean **two**. And should you express the desire to gaze at the **welkin**, who would know you meant the **sky**?

Becoming correct

A prescriptivist is a language expert who tells us how we should use words; a descriptivist is one who tells us how we actually do. They agree sometimes.

So the prescriptivist will insist that **alright** is not an English word, that the correct way to write it is as two words: **all right.** The descriptivist is probably closer to the right of it: alright is on its way to becoming a word.

The prescriptivist maintains that words like **access** and **impact** are nouns, names of things. But we all know and accept that we can **access** data and **impact** outcomes. So they have become verbs.

My fellow grammarians and I have insisted for years that using the word **hopefully** when you really mean **I hope** is an error and should be corrected. But I think we have to surrender; the language has changed.

Hopefully we can get used to it.

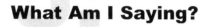

What Am I Saying?

It's probably impossible to overemphasize the importance of proof-reading. After you have thought, outlined, drafted, revised, edited, formatted, and rewritten—then it's time to proofread . . . and proof-read again.

If you wrote something like this . . .

"The manger has two no weather or knot too invest in professional development and four witch employees it mite be appropriate."

You might argue that your reader will know what you meant to say, despite the errors (none of which get flagged by spell check—see below). And you're right; I probably can figure out what you mean, but that's not all there is to communication.

Indeed, when somebody reads what you have written, consciously or not they draw conclusions about you. They have an image of you.

Part of that image is defined by the care you have taken in the presentation of your writing.

But it goes beyond image. A sentence like the one above tells your reader that what you are writing about is not that important to you, that it's not worth the time or trouble it might take to proofread.

Worse yet, it tells your reader that he or she is not very important to you—not really the message you wish to send.

Proofreading tips:

Experiment with different proofreading methods.

Some people can very successfully read their work, find errors, and fix them right on the computer screen. Others of us have more success making corrections on paper. Find out which one works best for you.

Read your work out loud.

Proofreading is not easy, especially proofreading your own work. You know what you meant to say, and often that's what you will read—even if that's not what you wrote. Reading aloud will help you to hear what's actually there. Getting someone you trust to read to you is even more effective. If something sounds "not quite right" to you, it probably means you have some editing to do.

The most likely place for a typo is in a heading or title.

Our tendency is to read the "small print" (references, citations, etc.) much more closely than we read headings. So make sure you give them an extra look before you hit "send" or "print".

Get as much distance as you can.

When you are confident you have finished proofreading and everything is perfect, put your work away for awhile (an hour, a day, a couple of days—the longer, the better). Then come back and proofread again. You certainly will find something that needs fixing.

Do not rely on Spell Check.

As we saw on the previous pages, Spell Check cannot be counted on to find incorrect words—unless they are misspelled. This little poem says it all:

Spell Czech

Eye halve a spelling chequer. It came with my pea sea.

It plainly marques four my revue miss steaks eye kin

knot sea.

Eye I strike a key and type a word and weight four it
two say

Weather eye wrong oar write. It shows me strait a

weigh.

Ass soon as a mist ache is maid, it nose bee fore two
long

And eye can put the error rite. Its rarely ever wrong.

Eye have run this poem threw it, I am shore your

pleased two no.

Its letter perfect in it's weight. My chequer tolled

me sew.

—Anon.

Words to Watch For - VIII

A longtime friend of mine (I hesitate to call him an "old" friend.) observed in an email the other day that he had corrected a colleague's use of "historical" when she really meant "historic". Thank you for the tip, Mr. F.

When you are preparing to sell your house, get ready for the realtor to walk through and point out all the odds and ends that you might want to fix up a bit or remove altogether. And she'll be right, but —seeing them every day—you got used to them; they're part of your everyday reality.

The same phenomenon occurs with word usage: we get so used to hearing words used incorrectly that they start to sound OK.

Here are a few of those.

Historical/Historic

A battlefield, document, or mansion, because they are important bits of history, are "historic" not "historical". The interest that an historian has in those things is "historical".

Factoid

Adding the suffix "oid" to a noun indicates that the thing being described looks like, but is not the same as, the original. So a "humanoid" in sci-fi looks like a human, but isn't. And a "factoid" is not a "little fact"; it's something masquerading as a fact.

Anxious/Eager

"Anxious," as its root would imply, means "worried," "filled with anxiety." Unless something is terribly wrong, you're "eager"—not "anxious"—to get home.

Verbiage/Verbage

"Verbiage" does not mean "wording." It's a disparaging word used to describe lots of unnecessary words. (It would be an insult to have your writing referred to as "verbiage.")

There is no such word as "verbage."

Expensive/Cheap

This one is pretty straightforward: it would not make sense to say that the **price** of something is expensive. The price is high or low; the thing is expensive or cheap.

#77:

Workin' It

Writing is hard work. Having an idea of what to do first, second, third, etc. tends to help get the work done and results in a finished product that does what it's supposed to do.

"Process" is one of those words that we hear and use all the time to denote lots of different things. There's "due process" and "process industry" and "processed hair" and "word processing." It's even a verb: with the accent on the "cess," we march to Mr. Elgar's "Pomp and Circumstance."

In general, though, the word is always about doing things in an order, Step 2 following Step 1, and so forth. But it's more than that: in a "process", Step 2 not only follows, but also depends on Step 1. So it is with what we call The Writing Process. And that goes something like this:

—Gather Information

—Outline

—Draft

—Rewrite/Edit

—Format

—Proofread

Step 1 of the Writing Process, **Information Gathering,** can be a multi-year research project or a 3-second quick thought. But we can't write without something to write about.

In Step 2, we put our thoughts into some kind of order using an **Outline**. This doesn't need to be a formal document with I., A.,

1., II., B, 2, etc. A quick list of topics will do nicely—just enough to remind us of what we need to cover and in what order. (NOTE: I know some superb writers who don't use outlines. They say that an outline feels confining to them. They know where they want to start and where they want to end up. Whatever works.)

Writing the **Draft** is Step 3. And the point of the Draft is to give us something to work on. Only when words and sentences get out of our heads and become objects on a screen or piece of paper can we move them around, find better ones, and make sure they say what we want them to say, in just the way we want them to say it.

Once we have a Draft on which to work, we get to the most important step: Step 4—**Rewriting and Editing.** This can mean several trips through the document, fixing, changing, rearranging, adding, and deleting. And this is the step that makes the difference between adequate and terrific.

When we are happy with the writing of the document, it's time for Step 5, the **Format**. In college courses, the format is often prescribed. But in general, it just makes sense to consider the impression your document will make, and to format it thoughtfully.

We've talked a lot in previous Wordworks about the importance of the final step, **Proofreading.** So we'll just note that all the work we put into the first five steps can be wasted if it looks like we didn't take the time and trouble to proofread.

ubject Index